A Likely Story

The Autobiography of Rodney Bewes

arrow books

Published in the United Kingdom by Arrow Books in 2006

1 3 5 7 9 10 8 6 4 2

First published in the United Kingdom in 2005 by Century
First published in paperback in 2006 by Arrow Books

Arrow Books Limited

20 Vauxhall Bridge Road, London SW1V 2SA

Random House Australia (Pty) Limited
20 Alfred Street, Milsons Point, Sydney,
New South Wales 2061, Australia

Random House New Zealand Limited
18 Poland Road, Glenfield,
Auckland 10, New Zealand

Random House (Pty) Limited
Isle of Houghton, Corner of Boundary Road & Carse O'Gowrie,
Houghton 2198, South Africa

The Random House Group Limited Reg. No. 954009

www.randomhouse.co.uk

A CIP catalogue record for this book
is available from the British Library

Papers used by Random House
are natural, recyclable products made from wood grown in
sustainable forests. The manufacturing processes conform to
the environmental regulations of the country of origin

ISBN 9780099415565 (from Jan 2007)
ISBN 0 09 941556 9

Printed and bound in Great Britain by
Bookmarque Ltd, Croydon, Surrey

To Bill Kenwright who saved my arse in the awful eighties.

For Daphne and Daisy and Joe and Tom and Bill.

Acknowledgements

Thanks to Dick Clement and Ian La Frenais
for permission to reproduce excerpts from
The Likely Lads scripts and screenplay.

Thanks also to Richard Weber for
permission to quote from
Whatever Happened to the Likely Lads?
(Orion; London 1999)

'Oh what happened to you,
Whatever happened to me,
What became of the people we used to be,
Tomorrow's almost over,
Today went by so fast –
Is the only thing to look forward to – the past'

Chapter 1

I COME FROM BINGLEY in Yorkshire. When I was six, we moved to Luton. If you come from Luton, then move to Yorkshire, you tell people you come from Yorkshire. If you come from Yorkshire and move to Luton, you tell people you come from Yorkshire.

Before I was four I'd experienced my first really embarrassing moment . . . On Thursday evenings 'the Man from the Pru' (the insurance man) called at our house in his trilby. He was considered a cut above. My mother would open the door, the Man from the Pru would smile and raise his hat. He collected a few shillings, wrote in his little notebook and went away.

On this evening I stood between them in my Rupert dressing-gown, holding my mum's hand.

'Mrs Bewes,' he said, 'I wonder, may I use your bathroom?'

Before my mother could answer, I ran to the foot of the stairs and shouted up as loud as I could 'Is anybody *on*?'

My mother gave me a look, a long look, and I knew I had made a huge social error. I blushed and backed away, confused thoughts rushing through my head.

★

I was always ill. There was a popular catchphrase from Northern comic Reg Dixon: 'Ee, I'm proper, proper poorly', that was me, until I was nearly twelve. I had asthma and, in winter, bronchitis too.

If you can't get enough air into yourself, it's very frightening. I'd be sitting very upright, straight back, hands on knees, trying to take deep breaths, shoulders heaving up and down, spitting, coughing, red-faced, scared. I had a 'puffer', not a little plastic gizmo that fits in your pocket like they have now, but a big red rubber bulb I had to press which had amber glass tubes coming from it, like the hookah pipe in *Alice in Wonderland*.

I was taken to Bradford for ultra-violet treatment. I found Bradford awfully big and dark, and couldn't think what people did in such big buildings. I had to take off all my clothes and put on some blue shorts: 'Get him stripped off and into a pair of the blue shorts provided.' With my little white body and dark Biggles goggles, I lay on a bed for hours under this lamp which had a kind of fishy smell. I can still smell that lamp now. I didn't like it, and I didn't like those shorts provided either.

At home, I would get out of bed and go and sit in an upright chair by an open window. I would look out and watch the other children, normal children playing in the street, playing with balls, kicking them or hitting them with bats. With my dad out at work, my mother working too and my brother at school, I spent hours at that window.

One night, I saw a car drive up and park beside the street lamp three or four doors down. It was a small family upright box, black, with spokes around the wheels. People climbed out, and a front door opened, light flooding into the street.

'Ow do? Nice to see yer, it's been that long . . .' Laughter, hugs, they went inside, the door closed. The street was dark, save for the lone street lamp, not very bright.

I crept downstairs and found what I wanted behind the air raid shelter in the back garden: a heavy length of chain. I crawled along the front gardens towards the dim lamppost beside the car. I threaded the chain in and out of the spokes of one of the back wheels, then, leaving plenty of slack, I wound the end around the lamppost.

Back at my window, I waited. Finally, the front door opened, light flooded out across the front gardens, and the people came out pulling on overcoats, waving goodbyes. Car doors slammed, the front door of the house closed. Engine started, dim headlights flickered as the car revved up.

It shot forward completely straight and upright for a few yards, then sparks flew and it was going along on three wheels and a bit of a rear axle. A terrible noise and, finally, it ground to a stop. The driver and passengers all got out. Doors opened along the street and the neighbours came out.

I climbed into bed and got right under the eiderdown and by the light of a luminous rabbit, I read for a bit, heart pounding.

Why did I do it? I honestly don't know. What awful guilt . . . no one knew it was me, and no one ever did, to this day.

My brother Geoffrey was five years older than me, tall and fair with blue eyes. He was healthy. He played football and cricket for the First XI. He went on to the grammar school where he passed exams.

He was also a hoarder. When you are little and your mother goes out to work, and you're home alone, you get to know the house pretty well. One day, I pulled open a drawer in my brother's bedroom, hoping to find a diary, or worse. I found his hoard. I moved a few shirts and there was row upon row of packets of Rowntree's Fruit Gums, hundreds of them. I wondered what would happen if I stole them all? Who could he tell? I did find a diary, with strange references to a girl called Zelda. There was stuff about her blouse. And I found, too, a copy of *La Vie Parisienne,* with pictures, and I found a pair of knickers, and they were *knickers*! Pink see-through with lacy bits.

Both my mother and father had originally come from Lancashire. They moved to Yorkshire because my father was offered a better job, and that is how my brother and I became two Yorkshiremen in a family of Lancastrians. So what, you might ask. Well, it's very important if you are a Yorkshireman.

My brother and I would go to stay with my grandparents in Alfred Street, in Lancaster, and there we re-fought the Wars of the Roses. Grandad in his chair beside the iron range would say 'Have you taught them to play cricket over there yet?'

'But Grandad, we invented it. It's a Yorkshire game, is cricket.'

'Don't be daft, they don't know how to play cricket over there, in Yorkshire.'

My grandad was a proper grandad. He worked in the mill and wore a flat cap and a knotted white scarf to save collar and tie, a waistcoat with a gold watch chain hanging down over his tummy. He wore boots, too, one with an iron brace from the heel to the knee to support an ankle, a bit of which 'was left behind on the Somme'.

My grandmother, Mary Agnes Bland, was the daughter of a stonemason in Lancaster. I can still see her, a little woman dressed in black, jet-black hair parted down the middle, making breakfast at the black iron range. I can smell the tomatoes frying in the big black iron pan now.

Grandad once took me to the circus and the clowns asked if any children wanted to come into the ring and join them jumping up and down on the trampoline. I got there first.

When we got back to Alfred Street, he said: 'He was out of his seat like a rocket and bouncing up and down with the clowns and soaring higher and higher, right up as high as the flying trapeze.' This story was told many times over the years and each time I would get higher and higher, and Grandad would say: 'And I knew from that moment . . .'

My father, Horace Bewes, was a clerk in the electricity show-rooms. Many years later, in the Sixties on *Late Night Line-Up* on BBC2, presenter Joan Bakewell asked me about my father. 'What does your father do?'

'He's a clerk, he's been a clerk all his life.'

She laughed.

'Why did you laugh?' I asked.

'Oh, you said it so proudly.'

Well, I *was* proud of him. He was a good man. No one ever said a bad thing about him. Oh, perhaps in my mother's eyes he was too unambitious and a pain in the shops, but . . .

I remember him going off to work on his bicycle, his cycle clips round his legs so his suit trousers wouldn't get oil on them from the chain. Off he would cycle to work, Saturday mornings too, his mac in a roll over his shoulder. An honest man, he couldn't tell a lie, and I remember he never sat down to write a letter.

'What are you doing, Dad?'

'I'm just *drafting* a letter, Rodney.'

Chapter 2

I WAS DEFINITELY GETTING worse. The doctor had a conference with my mother. 'I would advise a milder climate, Mrs Bewes. Move south perhaps?'

So we went to Luton. My father got a job in the electricity showrooms in Luton and lived in lodgings until he could find a house and send for us. When he did, he wrote home to tell us, after first *drafting* the letter of course.

Number 18 Hollybush Road, up a steep hill, was one of a circle of Thirties half-stucco, half-redbrick houses with curved Crittall windows and a cornfield stretching for miles behind.

As our things came out of the big furniture van, I stood waiting for my red tricycle. Another little boy stood watching as the bike was put on the pavement in front of me. He got nearer and nearer and I said to him, 'D'yer wanna go?' He solemnly threw his leg over and was away. Then he came back: 'Thanks, I'm Ieuan Harry . . . I'm Welsh.'

'S'alright, Rodney Bewes . . . Yorkshire.'

'That's a posh name, er, Rodney?'

'Yeah, well, we're not posh.'

'S'alright then,' and he became my best friend.

Because of the airport nearby, Luton was soon to be a target for German planes. I would hear the noise of bricks falling on bricks in an air raid, the strangest noise. You never forget it. And then there was the silence after a flying bomb cut out. Only the British could give a deadly weapon a daft name like doodlebug.

They sent me to Queen's Square Infants. Big A-frame Victorian school, with dark beams and partitions which were half-panelled, half-bevelled glass. There were hundreds of boys sitting cross-legged on the floor in short grey trousers, and the *noise*!

This is not going to last, I thought, and it didn't.

I was proper, proper poorly often, and sometimes . . . well sometimes, I just couldn't face it. So there I was, ill in bed again.

'I'm off now, will you be all right?'

'Oh yes, Mum, I'll be grand, you go.'

'You don't want the doctor?'

'No, I don't want the doctor.' I could fake it and who was to know?

I would sit up, propped up with pillows, and pull my knees up and tie my dressing-gown cord around the hump in the eiderdown. The cord had tassels that became my reins, and I was on a camel in the desert riding to the fort where the brothers in *Beau Geste* held out.

I made peep shows out of shoe boxes. A pin prick at one end, tissue paper at the other, and rows of painted scenery, a torch at the tissue paper end that lights up . . . 'a tableau'. I had cardboard theatres with characters that came on and off on slides. I wrote plays for them.

But I could never catch up at school. Times tables were a mystery to me, and I also fear I never learned the values normal children learn. As you will soon see, I have never had the same scruples, morals, a proper sense of right and wrong.

★

My father still rode off on his bike with his mac in a roll over his shoulders. He didn't have to go and be a soldier because he worked for the Electricity Board and was therefore exempt. He was a fire watcher, though, and I was very proud about that. Once the war came close, when a flying bomb fell in a field near Hollybush Road and the children ran to see it smoking. I longed for a piece to keep as a souvenir.

Then it was all over. There were parties in the streets with flags and jelly, and near us the prisoner of war camp got fuller and fuller. I saw them in their khaki jackets with big yellow patches on their backs, some Germans and many more Italians.

Ieuan and the other Hollybush Road kids had a swing, a thick old rope tied on a huge beech tree, down the hill near the POW camp.

Once an Italian POW grabbed Deirdre Birchwood and pulled her into the bushes. He had rather a wild look on his face. He pulled open his belt and undid his trousers and exposed himself to her. I ran into the bushes screaming and the others followed. Someone threw a stick and the man pulled up his pants and ran.

That evening there was a knock on the front door. It was a British Army officer with two military policemen in their red caps.

'Er, Mrs Bewes? May we come in?'

'Of course, come in, come in, put the kettle on, Horace.' (We were from the north.) The big military men balanced cups and saucers on their khaki laps.

It was awful at the Italian POW's court martial. The children were with their parents; Deirdre Birchwood in white ankle socks and buckle shoes and summer frock. The prosecutor asked me: 'Now, do take your time, sonny.' I resented that. 'Did you see the prisoner's penis?'

'Pardon?'

'Just take your time.'

I had no idea what he meant. They had to take me outside to explain in whispers.

There was a knock on the door on another occasion too. My mother opened it and on the top step was a man from across the green. It was dark outside. He stood uncomfortably in the light from the hall. 'Mrs Bewes, I don't know if you know, if you've been told anything about what your son's done today? Well, my Norman's got a bloody nose. I've never seen anything like it.' He was warming to his theme, sounding less uncomfortable and more angry. 'Some people have no idea. I mean some parents . . . don't know how to bring up children.'

My mother hit him. Hard. Not a punch, but a sort of swiping, flat-handed, swinging slap across the mouth that sent him flying back down our four front steps into our little front garden.

He got on to his feet slowly and with difficulty . . . 'You'll hear about this, you're not getting away with this. BULLIES, both of you!' Other front doors were opening now.

'Oh, get away you,' said my mother.

'I'll summons you for this.'

My mother slammed the door shut, went back into the living-room, pulled her travelling rug over her feet and burst into tears. 'Oh dear, oh dear.' Great sobs.

Dad came through from the kitchen. 'Now then, Bessie, what's up?'

'Oh, oh, he says he'll summons me.'

'Don't be daft, lass.'

'I'll be in court, oh.'

'Nay. . . .'

She blew her nose. 'A court appearance . . . for assault!'

'Now, see here, Bessie, do you think a grown man, like . . . er . . . the size of him is going to court to say a little lady like you hit him? Nay. I'll put the kettle on.'

She blew her nose again. 'Our Horace, I'll never hold my head up in Sainsbury's again.'

My parents went to old-time ballroom dancing and would come and say goodnight, my dad in a rather old double-breasted dinner jacket with shiny lapels, my mum in a long dress. 'Bring us back a balloon . . .' I said and after they had gone and my light was out, the darkness grew so intense and the walls of my bedroom would move outwards, forever into infinity . . .

I listened to the wireless in bed, under the covers with my luminous rabbit, through a pair of ex-army earphones. Plugged into the back of our wooden Forties wireless downstairs, the wires came up the outside of our house to my bedroom window and to my bed, where I listened to *The Vagabond King* and when Bruce Woodcock 'the Yorkshire Blacksmith' fought Joe Baksi for the heavyweight championship of the world and Bruce fought on for seven rounds with a broken jaw.

I sometimes worried that in a thunderstorm the lightning might find my wires and fry me under the bedclothes and I would be discovered later on, a charred little boy with earphones on, lit by a luminous rabbit.

A knock at the front door again. Bessie opened the door to see another army officer. 'Yes? What's he done now?'

'Er . . . Mrs Bewes?'

'Yes. Horace, put the kettle on! Come in here, sit down.'

'Thank you, I'm going around the neighbourhood asking if anyone is willing to have a German soldier for Christmas Day?'

Now, my grandad had left a piece of his ankle 'on the Somme' and

Uncle Jim had been at Dunkirk. That's two generations of my family in two world wars. My mother said, 'Oh, of course we'll have two, please.'

We had goose. We always had goose and I had a stocking with all the proper things in it – tangerines and a silver coin – piles of parcels even with rationing.

'It's Christmas,' Grandad said, 'we must not embarrass them by talking about the war.' The two German prisoners of war came and everybody talked about war. Grandad showed them his boot with the iron strapped just below the knee. 'Aye, left a bit o' me ankle . . . ON THE SOMME!'

The Germans really were called Fritz and Kurt, Fritz jolly and round, an ordinary working man with a red face, and Kurt tall and thin and strict, straight back, perhaps more like the German soldier I had expected to meet. They brought my brother and me a present each wrapped in brown paper, a tank with a six-inch nail for the gun for my brother, and a fort for me, a door-hinge for a drawbridge.

Everybody had a good time. When, years later, I was asked to write a piece for *TV Times* magazine about a family Christmas, I wrote about that one. Wasn't it an English thing to do? I think we are the only country in the world that would do such a thing, have a prisoner of war for Christmas.

My parents despaired at me ever having an education. They came up with the idea of a private school, a fee-paying type school, strangely called a public school.

'Would you like to go to a posh school?'

'Oh, well . . . won't it be a lot of money?'

'We'll manage somehow . . .' My mother set her heart on Tring, and I must say I liked the blazer. The first day came nearer and nearer.

I was scared and also excited. Then there I was, standing in the entrance hall of the school, all the boys with their sports things and bags and books. A master said to me: 'Boy, where's your shoe bag?'

I didn't have one. I thought, let's try and get to the end of the week.

I liked geography class once when the master asked a question and I was the only one who could answer: 'If the world is round like a football, how do we make a flat map of it?' I said, 'If you take an orange and peel it, all the segments are like the world before you start to make a map of it.' I got a 'Well done, bright boy!' But I didn't manage a whole term.

Another school was going to have me, St Albans, a better blazer and nearer, but I didn't even stay as long as at Tring. A third school sent me home because I laughed when the headmaster came in to announce: 'Gentlemen, stand up, a grave announcement . . . the King is dead.' I only laughed because of his face and the way he had said it, not for any other reason.

Chapter 3

I WENT BACK TO Yorkshire, to Ingleton, a special place of waterfalls and caves and mountains for a holiday with Auntie Edna, my mother's sister. She lived with my second Uncle Jim who was 'a character' and Uncle Norman who wasn't really anyone's uncle. He was a giant of a man who had worked in the slate quarries, and had a Yorkshire accent that made Michael Parkinson sound like Noël Coward.

Auntie Edna was tough. She had to be. They lived on the main road in a big stone house and opposite was The Mason's Arms, where you could always find my Uncle Jim.

Auntie Edna packed my cousin Michael and me off up to the high fells, camping. Up t'tops with Wordsworth's sheep, we had a little tent pitched by a torrent of a stream racing down from the waterfalls. We were just a good walk back to Auntie Edna's house for more beans and bread, but, still, we had a camp fire and the air was so clean, so fresh.

Suddenly I felt well, strong. I was twelve, so perhaps I was changing anyway, but the breathlessness became less frequent.

Dear Mummy, Daddy,

I hope you are very well, my ear is a bit better, the doctor has given me drops and a gargle for it. I shan't come home Saturday, I understand now that it was only homesickness that made me want to come home. I went for a walk with Michael on Sunday and we went right up into the Dales and I RAN home part of the way. RAN. I hope I am not breaking you but send the 10/- on Friday if you can.

Love and all the best . . .

Now I felt strong, I found myself at a secondary modern school, a twenty-minute bike ride away with my friend Ieuan. The school was a new building, round glass windows and an assembly hall with a stage at the end, where we did plays.

Our form master, Mr Tassie, helped me. He understood I could never catch up on sums, grammar and spelling, and I never have. Many years later, Sir Ralph Richardson would tell me to 'watch the consonants'. I didn't know what he meant.

I've never got over how odd it is that I'm an actor. I've been an actor for fifty years and I still think it's odd. No one from our family had been on the stage as far as I know. And how did Albert Finney become an actor with a dad who was a bookmaker's runner in Salford? Tom Courtenay's father used to paint the trawlers on Hull fish dock. I heard Tom on the radio recently, saying he couldn't possibly write a showbiz anecdote book: 'It'd be anathema to me . . .'

Well, that's what I'm doing now. You always were superior, Tom.

I started acting because I wrote a letter to the BBC. My father took a good socialist newspaper, *The Daily Herald*, and I read that a producer at Lime Grove was searching for schoolboys to be in a television series. I wrote at once and waited and waited. Would they reply?

The answer came in the form of a postcard, dated 27th November 1951 (my birthday), addressed to Master Rodney Bewes.

Would it be convenient for you to come to an audition at the BBC Studios, Lime Grove, Shepherds Bush, on Monday, 3rd December at 2pm? Perhaps you would let me know if you can not come.

Barbara Forrester

(Secretary to Joy Harrington)

Oh, it is convenient, I thought. I've waited a long time for this. All those days propped up in bed, all those days of being not so well, all those days of being proper, proper poorly . . .

My mother and I went to London. I wore my blazer with badges on both lapels, including my *Eagle* comic one. At the BBC Lime Grove studios, the uniformed doorman showed us to the lift and pulled the gates back with a crash. Forever afterwards, whenever I hear that noise, my mind flashes back to that December day when I was just thirteen and going to meet a television producer.

Joy Harrington and her secretary had tea and biscuits waiting.

'I'm casting a series, *Billy Bunter*. D'you know the books?'

'Oh yes, er . . . rather, the fat boy.'

'Do you *like* the books?'

'Oh yes, rather!' Actually, I thought them 'posh'.

'The whole point of today is to see you, I can't promise anything. I'm seeing hundreds of er . . . actors . . . you're certainly not fat, but you have a round face . . . perhaps with a little padding?' Flippin 'eck! Flippin 'eck . . . she's thinking of me for the main part, flippin 'eck. 'I want you to read for me, is that all right?'

'Oh yes, I can . . . Oh yes.'

'I'll cue you.'

There were piles of scripts everywhere, and over the tray of biscuits and tea cups we read scenes, and we read some more. 'You read very well,' she said after a while, and I thought she looked very thoughtful.

Then we went into a huge hangar of a studio, great black hooded lamps hanging from girders in the roof and gantries with chains looping down. There were microphones on long extending arms like giant giraffe necks stretching over the cameras which sat on telescopic stalagmites sticking out of the floor. And everywhere there were thick cables like giant black spaghetti. We stepped carefully over them as a lady came out to speak to Joy Harrington. I was introduced. 'Grace, this is Rodney Bewes, here to audition . . .'

'Hello, I'm Grace Wyndham Goldie, how do you do?'

'Oh . . . er . . .'

'Hope you get it . . . bye.'

On the train going home from St Pancras Station I thought of the studio and reading for a part, and who was Grace Wyndham Goldie? I didn't know she was a legendary producer of children's television shows such as *Muffin the Mule* and *Bill and Ben*.

Dad was doing his jobs in the kitchen when we got home.

'How did you get on?'

'I met Grace Wyndham Goldie!'

'Who's she when she's at home?'

'You know nothing.'

'Well, what did they say?'

'They said, they'll let me know . . .'

Christmas came and went and a postcard arrived.

Lime Grove Studios

Please could you come and see me again on Monday, 14th

January at 11.30am. Perhaps you will let me know if this is not convenient.

Joy Harrington

PS: I think you are not quite tall enough for Bunter, but you read so well, that I should like to see you again.

'I'm asked back, I'm asked back! Oh . . . flippin 'eck, FLIPPIN 'ECK!'

'Ay ay ay . . . language!' But Dad was smiling.

Back at Lime Grove Studios, lift doors crashing shut.

'I wanted to see you again, Rodney, you read so well. We have a short list. Actually, a short list of two! We have also seen a young actor, twenty-seven years old and awfully right.'

Four weeks later, Miss Harrington wrote to my mother to say that after a great deal of negotiating and discussion, they had decided they could not take the responsibility of causing a schoolboy to miss so much schoolwork.

Causing a schoolboy to miss so much of his schoolwork! There's irony for you, I thought. I don't suppose I had been to school for even two years in the whole of my thirteen years! I was bitterly disappointed.

Then one evening we sat down to talk, my mother and I. She had a strange expression on her face and a letter open on her lap. There was a hatchway through to the kitchen and, knowing something was 'up', Dad popped his head through. My mother adjusted the rug over her knees. I stood up again and assumed a favourite position, my back to the fire.

'How would you like to go to drama school?' she said.

'Oh, but how could we afford it? You mean in London?'

'Your father and I have talked about it and . . .' Mother passed me

17

the letter. It was from Joy Harrington, recommending PARADA, a preparatory dramatic school in Highgate, North London. It read . . . 'You may certainly mention my name when you write. Please give my love to Rodney and wish him good luck.'

While we were considering this, *another* letter arrived from Joy Harrington offering me a part in a playlet, written by a child, to play Jeremy in *The Mystery of Mountcliffe Chase*. Fee: nine guineas (£9.9s.0d), to include the services of a chaperone.

All my life I have never got over the thrill of being sent a script. All actors know the feeling. I've got a part! Someone's *thought* of me.

And even though this was just a small part, it was *work*. I was to be a real actor and so it was decided I would go to drama school. I wasn't quite fourteen.

Chapter 4

THE JUNIOR SCHOOL AT the Preparatory Academy to the Royal Academy of Dramatic Art, PARADA, was a detached single-storey building in the gardens of a big Victorian house in Highgate.

I commuted from Luton to Highgate and back again by bus to St Pancras Station to catch a train – a steam train, impatient, puffing black smoke and steam.

I always walked up the platform to see the driver and the fireman. 'My Uncle Ernest is a signalman, up north.'

'Oh yes, where's that then?'

'Morecambe. He was dive-bombed in the war.'

'Oh yes? Morecambe, single-line, isn't it?'

On my first day at drama school I was so in awe of the others, the children of professional people and actors, I didn't know what to wear, never mind how to speak proper, and oh, I was so provincial, so very north-country and very, very uneducated.

And so very badly behaved.

Madame Fedro was Hungarian or Polish, perhaps a White Russian? She had the most wonderful accent. Did she tell me she saw her husband's assassination? Saw him shot before her eyes?

She would lift up her black skirts to reveal black bloomers, the elastic just below the knee. She exhorted us to 'Swing from zee ip!' and she would curl her left arm into her waist so it became the rim of a basket and, with her right hand gliding across her body to the basket, she would pick out imaginary flowers. Then, her right leg raised up, she threw the flowers ahead of her like a farmer's wife scattering seed for the chickens, an elegant farmer's wife in black drawers, scattering seeds, to the loud exhortation of 'Zen YOU PICK IT UP . . . AND YOU STROW IT AWAY!' And she would dance across the room. 'You pick it up and STROW IT AWAY!' and I would follow across the diagonal in my black tights and ballet shoes, picking it up from my imaginary basket and strowing it away.

'Rrrrrodney! From ze shoulder, from ze elbow and from ze wrist, you pick eet up! and you . . .' Yes, and I would strow it away!

I loved dancing and dance, and do to this day, though I can't do it.

Monsieur Froeshlan was the fencing master. Now I'm getting somewhere, I thought, in my black tights, foil in hand. I went on to become quite good at fencing – which was important, because it stood me in good stead playing snooker later on.

Our singing teacher was Madame Guignard. Formidable and with an enormous bosom and not French at all. I had a good soprano voice, and I went on to have private lessons at her house in Bayswater, dark and Edwardian, where Madame Guignard lived with her spinster daughter. I sang:

> On a tree by a willow, a little torn tit,
> sang willow, tit willow, tit willow . . .

I liked that tune. It allowed me to indulge in pathos.

After six months, my parents talked about my staying in London rather than commuting. After all I was rushing towards being fifteen and I would be allowed to stay in London, they said, because of my health.

Janice Hardiman was in my class. She lived with her tall elegant sister Hillary and her mother in a white modern building in the Vale of Health on Hampstead Heath. The entrance hall led to a stairway down through two floors of the house and you descended the curved staircase, past a full-length tall statue of a naked girl at the bottom, sculpted by Janice's father.

Janice's black hair framed such a kind, feminine face, but she treated me as an idiot child. I can see her now, fifty years on, and hear her. 'Oh Roddy . . . you idiot . . .' she laughs, looks at me with a long questioning look. I bought a double-breasted blazer especially!

Janice's was my first party. It was in a studio with artistic people, brainy people, beautiful people. I was the youngest. I knew nothing.

I was asked, 'What do you drink?'

'Oh, gin . . .' I heard myself say. 'With water.'

I've never been able to drink gin since.

After a while I found a job to help pay my way, but I couldn't continue to live at the hostel where we were expected to be in by 10.30pm because the job was as a washer-up in the banqueting kitchens of the Grosvenor House Hotel on Park Lane, and the hours were from six in the evening until six the next morning.

I set about finding a flat in Hampstead, but first I had to swing it with my parents. I was fifteen, well, nearly. My mother consulted the family doctor who told her that after my having been a semi-invalid until the age of twelve she should thank heaven that I was now so happy and healthy. 'Let him have his head, Mrs Bewes,' he said.

The day I finally left home, a neighbour's van piled high with my things, there was quite a scene on the doorstep. My dear mother said, rather tearfully, 'Just remember, Rodney, it costs very little to be clean.'

With that advice ringing in my ears, I set off for 22 Belsize Avenue, a big front basement room with a bentwood rocker and a bed behind a screen. The rear basement housed Mrs Johnson, the housekeeper. Sometimes she cleaned my room, though it wasn't part of her duties. She was fond of me and used to keep an eye on me.

At Grosvenor House, I had to slip my job card into the time clock at six in the evening and go down, down, down to the staff room, long, scrubbed table surrounded by two benches against the wall either side, no windows. Hungarians and Czechs and all sorts in vests and assorted headgear were smoking and drinking tea. Should I tell them I was at drama school? That I was fifteen?

'Oh, I'm an actor.'

'What 'ave you bin in?'

'Telly. I've been on telly . . . I was in . . .'

'Shakespeare!'

It wasn't a question.

'Oh yeah, I've done Shakespeare. "This sceptered isle, this . . ."'

'No. We'll call you Shakespeare!' says Joe, the Polish foreman, 'Yeah, well come on Shake-es-pier, you come with me and I show you your place.' And down I went again, to be shown where I would work for the next two to three years, on and off. My place was a big sink with a wooden surround and scrubbed wooden draining boards either side to stack the piles of dirty plates. Twelve hundred dinner and twelve hundred side-plates.

Joe pointed to the huge aluminium shiny washing-up machine

behind me, as big as a room. 'It's the biggest in Europe! Bigger than the one at the Savoy. 'Ere we break more plates than the Savoy, or the Dorchester!' This, proudly.

'Then why do I have to stand at this sink if we've got the biggest washing-up machine in Europe, Joe?' I said.

'Your place, Shake-es-pier, is for the plates too bad to go through the washing-up machine!'

Early evening there wasn't much to do, but when it got busy, when things hotted up, that was theatre. I wore sandals, a vest and chef's trousers and a red spotty hanky at my neck to catch the sweat. When twelve hundred dinner plates all arrive back at the same time the heat rises.

The dirty plates were thrown into wire baskets, so they all stood up at an angle, thirty-six per basket and they all went through the great washing-up machine, continuously moving, steam belching out until the trays emerged from the other end, gleaming white and very hot, moving along slowly, until someone began grabbing the hot plates and throwing them on to the racks behind, swearing as hands hurt, and all the time Joe shouted above the noise, 'Keep 'em rollin' KEEP 'EM RRRrrolling!'

He was shouting and swearing and the waiters would join in too and the wine waiters and the chefs. I stood on my wooden grating in my sandals, a champagne bucket full of ice and fresh fruit salad at my right foot to keep me cool and keep me going, as plates were thrown my way, hot after having been through the washing-up machine but still dirty, and they would pile up in my sink or on the draining boards.

'Eh, Shakespier! Watch yer head!' as someone threw something my way.

Late at night, the coffee cups came back with cigarette butts and cigar stubs in the saucers. The cigarettes would unfurl in my water, the cigars floating on the top, unwrapping themselves. My sink stank. I stank.

The shouting was wearing thin now. The washer-uppers were clearing up, the floor being mopped. We had all the food you could eat, lovely bread rolls and lots of drink left over, half bottles of port or a bottle with a third brandy left, bottles of claret.

The banquet was over at 1.30am or two o'clock, but I couldn't knock off until six in the morning, so I would collect table-cloths smelling of breadcrumbs to make a bed for myself under a table, curl up like a dormouse and sleep till it was time for me to go.

After clocking off I would walk back to Hampstead along Oxford Street to the top of Tottenham Court Road, past the ex-army shop to Camden Town, past the art deco Carreras factory with its two huge matt black Egyptian cats guarding the entrance, past the closed Bedford Theatre to Belsize Avenue to my basement and then I would climb in through the side window into my little bed, behind a screen.

Then only a few hours later I would make some coffee and walk across the Heath to Highgate and PARADA, where I sat in the bay window of the large crowded room in the big Victorian house, trying to listen, but of course I was very tired.

The window was open. I was at the back. I slipped out of the window and walked to the Tube station to escape to the magical world of Soho.

Chapter 5

IN THE DOORWAY of the French House pub, half leaning out to see who was passing by, Iron Foot Jack gave me a signed postcard photo of himself. His left boot was built up and shod in iron. He wore a big black coat with a big black hat and said he had lost his foot to the sharks while 'pearl diving', though pearl diving was what everyone called washing-up in hotels and restaurants.

Inside the French House sat Imogen, white-faced and dressed in black; she always seemed to be there with a coffee and a glass of water. Was she an existentialist?

I would meet also art students from Central and St Martin's colleges around the corner, and sometimes from the Slade, and students from as far away as Camberwell, with its famous sculpture school. There were political groups in Soho and boozy groups and literary groups. The Anarchists had the Malatesta Club, where you could put money into a bowl on the counter for anyone without a job to help themselves. We drank cider and sang 'The Ballad of Joe Hill' from the International Workers of the World songbook. Intellectuals drank at the Swiss pub in Old Compton Street (Dylan Thomas had read poems there), and for serious drinkers, there were

The Colony, The Mandrake, Baz's and The Jungle. It was in a French café that I first met Marcus.

Bernard Kops, the writer and poet, had a second-hand book barrow on Earlham Street near Cambridge Circus, and Marcus used to sit at the stall and mind it for Bernard. After I'd met Marcus I used to help. I loved collecting the barrow early from the yard near Seven Dials then pushing it to Earlham Street.

Marcus and I admitted to being 'weirdies', because no self-respecting weirdy would call himself a bohemian. He dressed in period clothes. I thought I'd like that, so I wore striped City-gent trousers, tapered into drainpipes and sandals, a red shirt and black bolero waistcoat.

I met a girl at PARADA who became my first girlfriend. She came from Brown Edge in Staffordshire and her name was Violet Church. She had brown hair. I was fifteen and she was nineteen.

One night – was it in the autumn? – Vi and I walked home back down the hill to Belsize Avenue. She lived in a semi-basement near me, in a flat she shared with Clare a little further up the hill towards Haverstock Hill. Her basement front door was around the side, down some steps.

The night we went back, knowing it had to happen, it turned out we couldn't go inside because Clare was home. Light rain was falling, it was dark, and beside that door, the drainpipe and the dustbins, against a wet wall and standing up, we made love. Vi didn't know it was my first time.

A few nights later, in the Grosvenor House kitchens . . . 'Keep 'em Rrrrrollin'. Keep 'em Rrrollin'!!' I finished my work, piled linen table-cloths under a table in the Great Room and made my bed as usual. I rolled a couple of table tops around my little nest, crawled in and fell asleep, only to be wakened by Joe kicking me. He flung down the table tops with a crash and kicked me again. 'Eh! Get up, boy. There's work to be done!'

'Oh, Joe! Get off. I've done my place, 's'all finished . . . tidied up my sink, man.'

'You get up, boy!'

I got up, still very sleepy, and saw the three great chandeliers lit brightly above the room and at the top table, raised up high, were all my mates in their vests and neckerchiefs and assorted headgear and the table full of food and left-over drink: port, and brandy, decanters of claret and tall glasses of hock. In the middle of the table was an empty seat. Joe pushed me forward to the place of honour and I saw they'd even made a place card: 'Shakespier Bewes, Actor' and there in the centre of the table stood a cake with candles alight.

'You make a speech, boy!'

I couldn't, I was too moved, my eyes felt hot.

It was my sixteenth birthday.

I loved Vi Church so much it hurt. Our lovemaking was glorious. She was so feminine. I saw her in beautiful circles – her tummy, her breasts which were a wonder to me. I wanted her all the time.

One night, I remember, Vi was dressed in a black sweater and slacks. We sat on Hampstead Heath, overlooking the round pond framed with rustling willow trees, when she told me not to love her too much. It might only lead to hurt, she said. I felt so alone.

I knew then I had to get out of London, away from Soho friends and Hampstead distractions, and away from Vi Church, so I wrote to the Royalty Theatre, Morecambe, hoping for a summer job. I got a letter back. Assistant stage manager at a salary of £2.10s.0d per week. This would keep me occupied until I started RADA in the autumn.

The Royalty Theatre. A play a week. This was a real weekly repertory theatre, the scenery painted every week on canvas flats eighteen feet high and with a strong whiff of size that hit you as soon as you went through the stage door. I was ASM Small Parts . . . Assistant Stage Manager, play as cast, prompter, prop-finder, tea-maker. I had to find furniture and set dressing for the next week's play.

Of course the theatre had its own prop store, full of dusty picture frames, occasional tables missing a leg, long-forgotten pantomime props piled high, part of Cinderella's coach and an eight-foot comb. Dusty decanters and wine glasses, walking-sticks and canes.

I've loved sitting in the wardrobes of theatres where you can smell ironing. There are always girls there. The wardrobe mistress, covered in pins, her young assistant.

'You wouldn't do some washing for me, I don't suppose?'

'Oh Rodney, what are you like? You can see the girl's changing, trying on a costume.'

'Shall I leave?'

'I don't mind dear, I'm an actress.'

And most important of all, in the wardrobe the director never finds you. The producer doesn't know where you are. No one comes and asks you to do something. The wardrobe is usually at the top of the building and no one's going to come up all those steps. In other words, the wardrobe is a sanctuary.

One day, going propping, I knew exactly where to find a key bit of dressing for next week's Lancashire farce. I directed George, who drove an old blue furniture van, to Auntie Elsie's house.

'Auntie, this is George.'

'Ow do? Now you'll have a cup of tea.'

'Auntie, we're doing this great big drive around looking for stuff for next week's play.'

'Oh, yes?'

'Yeah, and it's a *really working-class play* so I wondered if we could borrow, only borrow mind . . .'

'What is it you're after?'

'I wondered, could we borrow that plaster Alsatian from your front window?'

We didn't get the tea and we didn't get the plaster Alsatian that stood rampant on a great green plaster rock between the net curtains of the front window.

Towards the end of August I had a part in a play at last. *Escapade* was about a couple whose children had run away from their public school. It was to be in this play that I discovered a theatrical pause, *the* theatrical pause.

Curtain down, end of Act One, I climbed the wooden ladder to pull the heavy ceiling up. I struggled with the great ropes on the dusty gallery, leaning out over a great void down to the stage many feet below. Then down two wooden ladders to the stage and around the back to the winch, putting my back in to it, turning the big handle and with a groan the stage slowly revolved until the second set was facing the curtain. Then up two wooden ladders again and back to the flies to lower the ceiling. I ran back down to the stage. Check time. Check props. Back up the staircase to call beginners for Act Two, then back in the corner to pout on the warm lights, tabs, and bars. Curtain up, Act Two.

The set got a round of applause. The scene: the Headmaster's study.

Jean Kent, up to do a guest appearance, has just asked the Head for an explanation as to why her sons are missing. The Head has said he has none, but knows that the boys' friend, Daventry, may be able to shed some light on the mystery.

Enter a rather dusty and not awfully smart schoolboy. The mother questions him about where her boys may be and why they ran away and there is rather a long discussion about the value of sending children away to boarding school . . .

DAVENTRY: Been reading a lot about anthropology recently, the theory is that the family is a natural unit, if you send the kids away, the parents may separate. Mine did.

I paused between 'parents might separate' and 'Mine did', the whole audience made this wonderful 'aaaaaaaAAAHHH' sound.

The theatre critic in the local Morecambe paper, after praising everybody else, said 'What a strange breathless performance from Rodney Bewes' . . . but he did go on to say I was 'memorable'.

I kept the pause in.

On the way back to London, I was dying to see Violet Church again. She had been away too, but said she would be back in London around the twentieth or thereabouts. I thought I would go to Euston to meet her. I wanted to surprise her. I wanted to see her walking down the platform with her suitcases.

I waited all day and most of the evening. I met every train. She didn't show.

I went back the next day and the next. Three days and long evenings at Euston Station. Waiting, waiting, getting lower and lower. I began to get to know the station staff. 'I've got an uncle who was a signalman, up at Morecambe you know.'

Over the next few days, when term started, I could never seem to get her on her own. She always seemed to be with Nigel Hunt. Was she going out with him? Well, he was her own age and he was fair and slim and nice-looking.

Then one night, Vi came to see me. 'Look, don't get upset . . . Perhaps, Rodney, we ought not to sleep together . . .'

'What?'

'Don't get upset.'

I pleaded, I shouted, I implored. I raved. Vi was crying, I was crying. I took her arm and together we went out, up through Belsize Village and through Hampstead Village up to the Heath. I fell on my knees. I said everything I could think of.

That night, alone in my room, I wrecked everything, smashed everything, I threw my lamp against the radiator, trashed the big dresser on the wall opposite the window.

I slept with Vi only once more after that, and then I felt I was just tolerated.

When she left for Birmingham, like a fool I followed. I hitched a lorry to Dunstable and then to Birmingham. Her mother opened the door. 'Oh, she's out, gone to the pictures. Do you want to come in?'

'No, I'll go for a walk, I'll come back.' It was pouring with rain. I walked and walked. When I went back, Vi opened the door.

'I thought it was you,' she said.

We sat in front of the fire listening to records. I stayed a couple of agonising days, then went back to Hampstead, my basement flat all wrecked.

A year or two ahead of me at RADA were Albert Finney and Peter O'Toole, Susannah York and Alan Bates. I don't suppose any of them knew who scrubbed the tables and prepared the vegetables in the RADA canteen on the top floor, because I had two jobs now. At dawn I would leave the Grosvenor House Hotel and walk along Oxford Street to Bedford Square and up Gower Street to RADA and before anyone else was there, I cleaned the tables in the canteen and peeled the carrots and potatoes.

I didn't go home for Christmas for the first time. I couldn't let them see the state I was in.

I was arrested on Hampstead Heath one night, in the early hours of the morning, being a cello. I was giving *The Swan* by Saint-Saëns, a very sad piece . . . in the moonlight.

The young policeman asked: 'What's all this then?'

'I'm playing Saint-Saëns' *Swan* to the . . . er . . . swans.'

'What swans? There ain't no swans!'

'. . . Oh . . . I'm a cello, you see.'

'You'd better come along with me.'

He handcuffed me to a red telephone box while making his calls. He asked me where I lived. I told him just up the road and he unlocked the handcuffs and let me go.

Then I got into trouble too at the end-of-term play at RADA. I was cast as an RAF pilot opposite a six-foot Canadian girl called Lian, whom I had to kiss. As the scene built up to the climax, I found I was enjoying myself. The moment arrived for the kiss and I'm afraid I got a bit carried away, the kiss got a bit too physical, and Lian said – as Lian – 'Goddam you Rodney, don't do that!' and slapped my face . . . hard! After the play, I was told that Sir Kenneth, the principal, would see me at ten o'clock the next morning.

So I found myself waiting outside Sir Kenneth Barnes's office. Surely they wouldn't expel you for a kiss? What would my mother say? The door opened and I went in. Sir Kenneth indicated a chair. He sat the other side of a huge Jacobean desk.

'Now, I hear you gave a girl a naughty kiss, on the stage?'

'Yes, Sir Kenneth.'

'Did you enjoy it?'

He stuck his hand out. Was this the end of the interview?

I jumped up amazed and . . . and YELLED. The chair was so close to the desk that if you jumped up suddenly, you nearly lost your manhood against the corner of the desk.

Sir Kenneth knew that when you sat down you would be too timid to move the chair back, and now he was laughing his head off. 'Hah, yes, well, don't do it again!'

I met Albert Finney in the canteen. 'Did you move the chair?'

'No, I didn't . . .'

'Aaaah . . .!'

The housekeeper, Mrs Johnson, became more and more worried about me. I must have looked awful because she said, 'I'm taking you to the doctor's – now!' and we walked up Haverstock Hill to her doctor. Mrs Johnson and the doctor talked in whispers. The result was that he made an appointment for me to see a psychiatrist. 'I've been very fortunate and managed to get you an appointment at the Tavistock Clinic to see a very eminent man. Normally you could wait six months to see this man, but you can go at the end of the week.'

He was called Israel. I was shown into this grey room. It was very quiet. I burst out, 'Look, I'm sorry I'm late, I hate being late, really. I got lost.'

Silence. He sat with his hands to his lips as if he was praying. 'Yes. Sit down, will you?'

I sat on an upright chair facing his desk and the window. The desk had nothing on it. It was a bare room. Silence.

'Yeees?'

Long silence, after a long time, perhaps fifteen minutes.

'Yeees?'

Silence.

'Vot are you thinking about?' He had a mid-European accent (of course).

I answered truthfully. 'I'm thinking about the pattern on the carpet.' It was a plain grey carpet. 'I mean the shadow of the casement window on the carpet. The sun is making the window appear on the . . . er . . . carpet . . . except it's longer . . .'

Silence.

'Yeeees . . .?'

Silence for perhaps another fifteen minutes.

'That is all today. Please come again to see me, yes? You will come next week? Yeees?'

He opened the door. In the corridor I leaned against the wall, exhausted. I was given an appointment card for the following week.

I then walked down Portland Place looking at all the fabulous Adam doorways and on to the lovely Nash church. I sat at the back of that church and thought, now I'm going to a psychiatrist.

The washer-uppers at the Grosvenor House thought it was very funny. 'Ere Shake-es-pier's a looney just like us!'

Chapter 6

DAD WAS THE quietest of gentlemen. With his mac on his shoulder, he went off to work at the Eastern Electricity showrooms these days in a little blue Mini. He also went off to NALGO conferences with his mates Albert Northrop and George Blood to Blackpool or Bournemouth and they got up to all sorts of mischief.

'Well, Horace,' said my mother. 'Did you have a nice time?'

'Oh, all right, you know, one conference is much like another. I've brought our Rodney a stick of rock.'

But when we were alone. 'Ee, we had some fun, shut the door lad, and let me tell you. George Blood and I dressed up as maids, you know, chambermaids. And we went and hoovered Albert Northrop's room with him in bed, at one o'clock in't morning!'

'Ee, Dad, you'd best not tell me mother!'

Neither did I tell them about my visits to the Tavistock Clinic.

Mr Israel said, 'Yeeees . . .?'

'Oh . . . nothing.'

Silence.

'Hmm?'

I did my National Service.

Everyone talked of ways of getting out of it. My Soho friend John Upton got out of it in a beautifully subtle and funny way. At his medical test he refused to undress. Now, John was a well-built lad. He went all over the country wrestling against great big 'Black Bombers' and 'Hooded Assassins'. He could look after himself, but now strangely, it seemed he couldn't take his clothes off in this room full of men in white coats staring at him. 'Come on son, there's only us here, no need to be shy.' Slowly, very slowly John took off his jacket, slowly one shoulder at a time, the buttons on his shirt took an age, one at a time.

'Now, come on sonny.'

Slowly undoing the zip of his trousers, still holding his unbuttoned shirt across his powerful chest.

'We haven't got all day, lad . . . we've seen it all before.'

John let his shirt fall open and his trousers dropped to the floor. Everyone was looking. He was blushing deeply, He was wearing black see-through camiknickers, black bra, fishnet stockings and a suspender belt.

'Get out!' and he did.

Some swore by eating a bar of soap. 'You just stand there frothing at the mouth.' Albert Finney got out because he sat cross-legged on his bedside locker in his hut with a daft expression on his face, didn't eat and kept fainting. He was out in eight weeks. Tom Courtenay got out of it when a psychiatrist put him down as 'temperamentally unsuitable'.

I had been proper poorly in bed while others played or went to school, and then such a dunce at PARADA. Israel told me he could get me out of it by writing me a note, but I wanted to do National Service to conform, to be like other lads. I wanted to prove that I was normal.

RAF Cardington in Bedfordshire began with a week of queuing – to eat, to do your teeth, to get kit and to go to bed. You were called airman and had to 'ave an 'aircut, and the barbers took great delight in their work. Everyone emerged looking the same.

When the train stopped at Wilmslow Station the shouting began.

We were shouted into lines four abreast. We were 'orrible' airmen and the 'worst shower' they had ever seen. We were marched up the hill in the dark and it began to snow. We had our kitbags on our shoulders and some of us began to wish they weren't so full. 'Left 'ight Left 'ight, swing them arms.' Up the hill we went, the snow swirling around, then 'left wheel' past the brightly lit guard house. The RAF Police stood on a veranda looking down on us. We marched past rows of identical huts and before you could say 'Squad 'alt' we were in our hut, twenty-eight of us around an iron stove, trying to get warm, red faces.

Most had never been away from home before. One lad had been to university and was set to become a barrister, another was a docker from Glasgow, and another a midget bodybuilder. 'Ughie' Crockett, in the bed opposite, was called 'Ughie' because he was Scottish and always on about Drambuie. That first night in our hut, I could see the little door of the stove glowing, and I could hear someone sobbing, hoping he couldn't be heard. 'Shut it, will yer? For f***s sake. Let's get some f***g kip.' That was Dave, our docker from Glasgow.

Corporal Patterson woke us the next morning. He was 'our' corporal – weren't we lucky? And now we were to get washed and get our 'irons' and get to breakfast. Our 'irons' were our knife and fork and spoon. After breakfast Corporal Patterson told us to wash our irons and then he would show us what to do with them. He also showed us how to fold everything nicely, blankets, sheets, socks, everything on our beds for inspection, including our 'housewife' – a sewing kit in a little canvas roll, and a plastic thingy with a slot in it for polishing brass buttons. At the end of the hut was a private room, Corporal Patterson's room. So he was never very far away, which was a comfort.

On the parade ground one poor lad from our hut, called Bruce, just couldn't march. Also he was a little on the short side, so he really stuck out. His problem was that when his right leg went forward, so did his right arm. Then left foot went forward with his left arm. Eventually he was discharged. If it was a ruse it was brilliant, because it is very hard to march like Bruce marched.

Up and down the rest of us marched, day after day. The uniforms began to fit, the boots to resist less. We wore a beret and battledress top, trousers tucked into webbing gaiters. The webbing gaiters had to be blancoed, as did our pack straps and our belts, and our backpack, large, and side pack, small, and the little pouches at our fronts for bullets and other useful things, oh and I nearly forgot the strap on our guns. 'Never let me hear you call it a GUN! Never! It's a f★★★g RIFLE, got that?'

I was often in trouble on the parade ground. A lot of the time it was because I was in a daydream or just because of the look on my face. In the RAF this look was called 'dumb insolence'. I didn't mean it to be.

'You are on a flaming charge, Shakespeare!'

'What? What've I done?'

'Oh nothing yet, get that rifle above your 'ead and round the field three times, right!'

'Yes, Corporal.'

'And get that look off your face!'

The station warrant officer ordered me to 'Ave an 'aircut, laddie.' And three days later we were on a big parade and the station warrant officer stood before me.

'I'll see you in my office after the parade, Bewes!'

'Sir.' Oh dear, what now?

In the office, 'At ease.' Feet apart, hands behind your back as the SWO circled me.

'What would you say if I was to tell you . . . you are dirty? What would you say if I was to call you a dirty airman? What would you say if I told you I intend to telephone your mother?'

'Er . . .?'

'Don't you speak. Don't you open your mouth. I'm going to ring your mother. I know her name, it's Bessie, isn't it? Don't you speak. Don't speak to me, and I shall say to her, I shall say, Mrs Bewes, Bessie, this is your Rodney's station warrant officer speaking. I'm ringing you up to tell you your son is dirty, he's a dirty airman on parade! And how is she going to feel, eh? And I shall tell Bessie how I know her son Rodney is dirty. How I know he doesn't wash behind his ears of a morning. I know he doesn't, 'cos three days ago (now warming to his theme and loudly) HIGH HORDERED HIM TO AVE A AIRCUT AND THIS MORNING HIGH SAW HA HAIR IN IS HEAR HOLE!!'

'Oh, but. . .'

Up at six to clean my kit, dash to the cookhouse for breakfast, dash back to billet (hut). Don greatcoat, rush to armoury, grab rifle, polish bayonet. 'Right Dress, Quick March, Present Arms, Quick March, Halt, Fall Out'.

I would get very low and lonely. Twenty more months seemed a long, long time. I told myself I ought to think how much good it was doing me, how it was helping me to get things into true perspective and what a nice ordinary lad I would be.

Chapter 7

I COULDN'T WAIT TO get to Soho and see Marcus and my weirdy friends with their weirdy clothes. I had on my tight striped trousers and a smock, a washed-out fisherman's old blue smock. The date was Monday 9th April 1956. How do I know that? It was in all the papers, that's why.

I got up at twelve noon and Marcus's landlady made a cup of tea. I took a cup to Marcus in the bath and found him wondering whether to keep his wispy beard or not.

We decided to go to see Marcus's friends at the Camberwell School of Art. We walked to Whitehall to get the bus to Camberwell and saw that Big Ben was covered in scaffolding. Could we? Shall we? We said we'd be back this way that night.

We had a great afternoon at Camberwell and that evening in Henekey's pub with Lynne and Brian who were at Camberwell School of Art, we told them about seeing Big Ben that morning. 'Course we would need a trophy for the top.' Lynne took off her panties and handed them to me across the table. 'Here, put these on Big Ben.'

I shoved them in my pocket. We left the pub about ten thirty and said goodnight. We'd had a few drinks, but we weren't legless. We caught a bus back to Big Ben.

Now the problems began. How to get in over those railings? We looked at the statue of Boadicea driving her chariot with scythes on the wheels and I saw down there in the dark on the water, a small boat, a dinghy, no oars. Marcus's pale face said 'Come on', and we climbed aboard and cast off. The water was very calm. I paddled with a folded newspaper. We glided under Westminster Bridge. As we came out from the bridge two girls stared down at us and waved, and we waved back.

We tied the boat to a bronze ring in a great bronze lion's head, very handy for some stone steps on to what I later learned was Speaker's Green. At the foot of the tower lay piles of sandbags and, standing on these, we could reach up to the first scaffolding bars. The climb had begun.

For a couple of hundred feet there were no ladders, and the next scaffolding pole was always at chest level, so you had to pull yourself up on a vertical pole to get your feet on the next horizontal pole.

It was very quiet up there, the clock face getting nearer, but then, like a slumbering giant with asthma, it stirred inside and then boomed, and we nearly fell off.

Then up and up and there was Marcus, so enthusiastic: 'I mean, man, we are actually climbing Big Ben! . . . oh, oh, oh, I mean, man!' There were ladders and suddenly we were at the top. It was just like mountain climbers must feel.

The view was breathtaking. All the lights and the river, silver in the moonlight. There was actually a little platform above the weather vane, and a lightning conductor sticking up above that. I hooked Lynne's panties over the lightning conductor, and we heard . . . what was it?

We looked down towards Whitehall and, oh yes, of course, police sirens! We saw vans and police cars, van doors opening and policemen pouring out and on the river, police launches, searchlights up and down the Houses of Parliament. We stood and gawped. The beams of the searchlights were criss-crossing each other, and dogs were barking . . . according to one newspaper report, there were over a hundred policemen, seven squad cars, and two dogs with their handlers.

Remember the two girls on the bridge? They had called the police and the newspapers. They were two nurses going off duty. Parliament was due to reassemble within a few hours, though we didn't know this of course. Neither had we given much thought to Cypriot threats to bomb the Houses of Parliament.

We saw Parliament Square cordoned off. Perhaps it was time to climb down. It was too dangerous to cross the clock face, so we found a hole in the masonry and there we could just make out stone steps going down and down in the darkness. The clock struck two. We descended until we could see light and we were on the ground, fresh air and people shouting. I was suddenly calm. After all, it was just a laugh, only a prank. But Marcus ran for the great iron gates on to the approach road to the bridge. He climbed the railings and was near the top when he was grabbed by a big burly policeman and pulled off, to much shouting: 'I've got one! Here's one of them.' Others joined, more shouts and I saw Marcus, arms bent behind his back, led away.

I rolled under the pile of building materials, sandbags and timber but a boot descended on my arm. I was frogmarched to a police car.

Then I was in Canon Row, the Metropolitan Police station. Uniformed policemen gave way to CID who thought I was a bomber. They took my few possessions and searched me. Then I was locked in cell number three . . . alone . . . calm . . . scared. I wondered what had happened to Marcus. Then I heard him, from the next cell.

He was in number four and we could talk through a metal grille in the base of the wall.

'Is that you, Rodney?'

'Yeah, you all right?'

'Yeah. Don't tell them anything. They say you're queer, that you're a drug addict, a drug addict poof! They ask you if you are a fully paid-up resistance fighter for the Cypriots.'

The door opened and a policeman took me up a spiral staircase, into the office of my interrogator, a little man in a brown suit.

'Sit down, Rodney, do you smoke? Cigarette?'

'No, thank you. Look. It was only . . .'

'Shut up, don't talk now. Listen to me. We know a great deal about you, about your private life. I've spoken to your mother, er . . . Bessie, isn't it?' (I've been here before, I thought.) 'Naturally, she is very upset. Naturally. I want you to tell me in your own words who put you up to it. Understand? Start at the beginning and tell me everything you did tonight.' He spoke quietly and even a little kindly.

Laboriously he wrote down everything I said in longhand. Then he got up and was standing over me, waiting I thought for me to sign my statement, but instead he tore up the pages into little bits that he threw in my face.

'You're lying! You're a f***ing liar, aren't you? You're with f***ing EOKA, aren't you? I want to know who put you up to it? Who? You tell me, you bastard. I know you are in the RAF and you are going to be court-martialled for this.' He threw my RAF identity card 2765108ACI Bewes R on the desk.

'You are going to do many days in Shepton Mallet military nick for this, and it won't be like a cushy civil prison, mate. That's if you aren't EOKA or anarchists or effing poofters, in which case I will personally see you are taken to the effing Tower and shot!'

There was a knock on the door, I swivelled round to see a policeman holding up Lynne's panties. It was nearly five o'clock. The CID man looked from me to Exhibit A and back again. I was taken back to my cell.

'Marcus, are you there?'

'Yeah, you were a long time. Did he call you a poof, a drug addict?'

'No, an EOKA terrorist.'

'Oh, not so bad then.'

The door opened again and we were led out to a police car and driven back to Marcus's room in Millman Street. The CID man came to search the flat. Having found no bombs he threw down my RAF ID card and said: 'You! You'll be hearing from your commanding officer!' and they were gone.

All the excitement, all the fear turned into relief. Soon I was passing the guardroom with seconds to spare before my pass expired. I had a bath and a haircut and pressed my number one uniform with the marksman's crossed rifles on the right cuff. Then it was time to see the squadron leader.

He began quietly, but he was furious. 'You have let ME down, ME! Understand? You have let this station down. You have let the RAF down.' He was getting louder now. 'You have let the flag down! The country! You have let Great Britain down, her Majesty the Queen, you have let her down. You have let . . .'

Before he could add the world and the universe, the station warrant officer came in. 'The CO will see him now, sir.'

The squadron leader wanted to come too but the CO wasn't having that.

'You can leave us now, squadron leader.'

'But he's let . . .'

'Please.'

And then when we were alone, 'Sit down, at ease, and try to tell me everything, will you?'

'Thank you, sir. I wouldn't waste your time but I think it will be in the newspapers and I wanted you to hear it from me first.'

'Thank you.'

I sat down and told the story, then when I got to hanging our trophy on the top of Big Ben, I think I saw the hint of a smile. I finished.

We sat in silence for a while, then he leaned forward on his elbows across the desk, his chin resting in the palm of his left hand, his right hand playing with his moustache. He said, 'Rodney, I have a son at Oxford. I wish he had the spunk to do something like that.'

Chapter 8

IT WAS IN ALL the papers, but sadly, no photograph of Lynne's knickers flying high over Big Ben. According to *The Times,* they were removed by police at 4.15am. Reports ranged from 'Black Lace Panties on Big Ben' to 'An Article of Women's Underclothing adorns the Mother of Parliaments'.

One month later I was in trouble with the squadron leader again. On a charge. My crime: an untidy room. Am told to do 'fatigues' for four hours.

Winter was upon us now, and I was low. I ran outside and shouted hate into the night, tears pouring down my face. I went inside and sat on my bed and thought of that familiar walk from Gower Street, from RADA through St Giles Circus, then Soho Square and Greek Street to coffee in Old Compton Street.

My birthday came and went. I was nineteen, and on guard again. I was wearing long underwear for the first time in my life, the winds icy cold. Ridiculous to make a lad like me walk about in the dark, and in this cold with an old unloaded gun on his back.

And on my last leave I was beastly to my Mother. She'd been so good to me with parcels and letters and the odd, very welcome, three pounds. I went home on Christmas leave, and well, the sad fact was

I felt out of place. I seemed to get in everyone's way and in the evening I drank too much and laughed too loud . . .

I was told to shut up.

I threw up my arms and said, 'In your own HOME!'

I had a new suit for my test for readmission to RADA. Pale green cavalry twill. I decided to wear my woven tie Marcus gave me. It was a very hot day, and my mother insisted on coming up to London. I left her in the coffee house in Store Street and walked around the corner to Gower Street, and the test. I felt so terribly nervous, more so because I had brought my mother with me.

After the audition, I went back to Mum. 'Well thanks for coming. I've got to go and see some friends. Is that all right?'

'Oh, I thought perhaps we might go to Selfridges and then have lunch?'

'Look, Mum, you do understand. I've . . . I've got to go.' And I left her.

I had met a girl, a painter, with the strangest, fierce unhappy face. Pat Brown. She had a fabulous flat in Camberwell which she shared with Ann, a music student. I thought it was heaven. It was a council flat in a great tower block with Pat's room full of long paint brushes in tall glass jars and canvases and that smell of oil paint.

That night I asked Pat to a film. After the film, Pat and I sat for hours in her room in the light of one candle stuck in a bottle. We were holding hands. She told me she wanted to go to the Slade. I was playing with the wooden beads around her neck and let my hand fall to her lap. We both laughed, it was so terribly obvious, and then we kissed, laughing, a beautiful kiss, as if we had both been waiting for that kiss all evening. We undressed and went into the bathroom together holding hands and did our teeth together holding hands and laughed and went to bed. I got up in the morning and bought eggs, bacon, tomatoes and pork chops.

Then we went to the Whitechapel Gallery. Pat said she was tired. I thought I should never be tired again. I took her to see the book barrow and later to The Star for spaghetti and The Duke's for cider and to 100 Oxford Street for trad jazz, oh, I know how to sweep a girl off her feet.

Was I falling again? I dared not say 'love', because Pat had expressed a strong dislike for the word.

I was still on leave, staying with my parents, when Mum announced she wanted to come to the PARADA reunion. It was two days before I was due back on base. 'Congratulations,' she said 'of course I knew you'd pass. I said to your father, "Horace," I said . . .'

'Why, why do you want to come to the reunion?'

'Well, dear, I've met so many of your friends, that nice Violet Church.'

'Look, I'm, well, going straight back, er, like now.'

'Can't you wait, Rodney and travel up with me? I can leave early.'

'I have to meet someone.'

'Someone you would rather take to the PARADA reunion? Rather take than your mother, your own mother?'

We are near tears now. I want to take Pat.

'I can't face the journey on my own. You've spoilt it for me now, anyway.'

'Well, look, Mum, you must do what you think best.' I caught the train to London, alone.

I went straight round to Pat's.

There was a girl naked on the bed, and Pat was at her easel. I was afraid what she would think of me in my green suit. I needn't have worried, she smiled at me. I wanted to take her to the PARADA 'do'. She wanted to stay in, but eventually she put on a smart black dress, grey coat and red shoes. I introduced Pat to Vi Church and when it was all over, people saying their goodbyes, I led my mother to the front door.

'Look, I can't travel home with you, I have to be in London tonight. I go back to camp tomorrow.'

'But what about your father? He's expecting . . . he'll be bitterly disappointed.'

'Look, I have a very strong reason to want to be in London tonight.'

'That girl, I suppose?'

'That girl has a name, Mum, she's called Pat.'

'She looks odd to me. Her eyes are very close together.'

'Mum, it's important to me to . . .'

A mistake.

'More important than spending your last night with your parents? Your parents who've sacrificed so much so that you could go to theatre school? We went without, so that you . . .' Forgotten how I worked nights, how I was self-sufficient, how . . . tears now, and she got her coat and left. She was walking away up Shepherd's Hill in the rain and I let her go. I went inside, back to Pat and felt wretched.

Back at the base I was counting the weeks to demob. I couldn't wait to get back to Pat and RADA.

But two days to demob a long letter from Pat arrived. She said she'd been seeing Ted, a ghastly boring bisexual. 'Don't think my feelings for you have changed, but expect yours have for me now you have read this letter . . . risk I had to take. Pat.'

I felt so angry with her for making me feel this way. I didn't want all the difficulties with women again. I'd had enough . . .

Back at RADA. Madame Fedro is still teaching movement, still lifting up her skirts to the height of her black bloomers and, 'From ze shoulder, from ze elbow, from ze wrist, you pick eet up and strow eet away!' But, there's no one I know among the students. It's a very different atmosphere, and they all seemed a lot keener.

One Monday morning, I was sent home. They said I looked dreadful. I had got another job to support myself. On the dilly! On Piccadilly, in a coffee bar, called Pronto, facing Eros, we did beefburgers and cheeseburgers and lemon meringue pie. Beefburgers on an oblong hot plate, flip them over with the onions and hotdogs rolling around on shiny silver rollers.

Up a little staircase was our rest room with a half-crescent window overlooking Piccadilly. Rajah, studying to be a doctor, came up the stairs with his bucket and mop. Rajah was a Sikh and proud in his turban. 'Oh, my God! Oh, my God!'

'What's the matter, Rajah?'

'One of the working girls has peed herself and I've had to mop it up. Oh, my God . . . oh, my God!' I can hear him now and see the look on his face.

The whole of human life was there, girls on the game, their ponces, rent boys, and small-time crooks. Maybe I had met a better class of person washing up at the Grosvenor House, but I enjoyed Pronto. I wore a double-breasted chef's jacket with white cloth buttons, a white neckerchief and a funny white cap on the side of my head.

On my twentieth birthday, I was finally expelled from RADA. My mother was very shocked. She wrote to the principal, Mr Fernald, that I was tomorrow's Laurence Olivier. He wrote back: 'Rodney's talents should be channelled into another profession.' In other words: give it up.

I started writing off to repertory companies: 'I am five foot eight inches tall with dark hair. I was on children's television at an early age in minor roles. I enclose a recent photo and a stamped addressed envelope.' In the meantime, I stood at the doors of Pronto in my white jacket and funny hat on the side of my head and looked up at the night sky above Piccadilly and asked myself what I was doing.

The girls on the game had parties in their Euston flats, and sat around telling stories and reading comics. Even the youngest were old before their time, like poor children in Dickens. They did it because they had children at boarding school, or the husband had gone off, or just because it was 'easy'. Well, they all said it wasn't so easy the first time, then after that it just bored them.

In those days there were a lot of girls from Pronto to Curzon Street openly plying their wares, as subtle as an air raid. Carrying their little dogs, wearing fur stoles and lots of costume jewellery, including a little gold chain around the ankle, they would sashay into Pronto with their ponces and sit on a high stool. Rajah eyed them doubtfully. Ciggies would be lit, and there would be laughter and a few tears.

Mostly they kept themselves to themselves, except Iris and another girl this one particular night:

'Don't you mention my name!'

'Who wants to mention your farkin name?'

And that was all it took. I had seen some fights in the RAF, but this one made me sick. Outside, a crowd gathered in seconds, and we only just managed to get them out through the doors.

'You, you're nothing but a cheap taxi whore!'

No one intervened as high heels became weapons, then Iris lifted the other girl off the pavement and smashed her head against a lamppost. A great roar of disgust and encouragement went up. Only then did the ponces go in and pull them apart, and two policemen, who had been watching, moved in to disperse the crowd.

My mother and Auntie Edna came to see me on one of my breaks, and I took them to the lovely Italian in Windmill Street – Spaghetti Bolognese, 1/9d – and who should walk in but Iris!

'Oh, 'ello Rods, love, 'ow are yer? What farkin weather! Is this your mother? Coo, don't you look alike?'

'Oh, er, yeah, and me Auntie Edna.'

'Oh, ever so glad to meet yer. We've 'eard so much about you, Mrs Bewes. Bessie isn't it?'

Then in comes Lee. 'Ellow Rodders, pet. 'Ow's yer love life? This ain't your muvver?'

Then Rita. Each one seemed to be wearing the same fox fur stole and carrying the same little dog, and each one had a hint of gold around the ankle. 'Hello love, this your mother? He's ever such a nice lad. No side. Shame about him being kicked out of RADA.'

My mother gathered herself for: 'Oh, we don't care about RADA, he's well shot of RADA! Several reputable repertory companies want him.'

Auntie Edna looked astonished. 'That's told 'em, Bessie!'

My last night at Pronto the girls brought little leaving presents and promised to come and see me in a play at Watford. 'S'on the farkin Tube line, innit? We're all coming, love . . . promise!'

'Here give us a kiss, lots o' luck, love, s'only socks but you need socks, don yer?'

Iris gave me some underpants with lipstick kisses on them. 'F'when yer in Noël Coward, dahling!' Much laughter all round.

Rita gave me a wonderful tie with a bathing beauty stretched out on it, hands behind her head, smiling invitingly.

One repertory company did want me. The Palace Theatre Watford. I didn't tell them I was expelled from RADA. I was assistant stage manager, small parts, play as cast, five pounds a week.

Then with two weeks left at Watford, I wrote to Harry Hanson who ran lots of repertory theatres in the North and arranged to see him.

Mr Hanson lived in a bungalow near Hove. I turned up at his door and he took my coat. I followed him into his front room where he gave me tea and said, 'Now what have you prepared, Rodney?'

I stood on the long carpet at one end of the living-room. I was required to do two pieces, one classical, one modern. Then when I had finished, he said, 'Sit down, sit down . . . Now, what have you done?'

How many times was I to answer that question? I said, 'I've been on television and I've been in the theatre since I was fourteen, I shall be twenty-one in November.'

Mr Hanson suddenly looked very serious and leaned forward in his chair. 'Can you SPARKLE?'

No hesitation. 'Oh yes, I can sparkle.'

'Go on then, SPARKLE.'

Lost now and uncomprehending. 'Oh I can't just do it in, er, a room!'

And that seemed to satisfy him. He fetched my coat and said: 'You are a very promising young man . . . be in touch, I'll let you know. Goodbye.'

Chapter 9

I ALSO WENT FOR an interview with a producer called Michael Gover, in Eastbourne. He took me to the pub and introduced me to the company who were having a break from rehearsals, then he introduced himself. 'And I'm God!' He talked very quickly and wore a silk cravat, insisting I stay and see the play. 'I can offer you six pounds per week, but you must see the play tonight.'

'Er, six pounds? I've been in the theatre since I was fourteen, and . . .'

'Oh, all right, seven pounds a week.'

'Oh, thank you.'

'What you will see tonight is standard. I insist on STANDARD!' He thought he was Noël Coward.

After the play we met up again in the dress-circle bar.

'Well? And what did you think? I told you we set a very high standard.'

'Oh well, it was lovely, er, very good.'

'And . . .?'

'And . . .?'

'The standard?'

'Oh, very high . . . Very high.'

In the first week I was sent out to find a drinks trolley for a production. After walking miles and a great deal of hassle, I found a beauty, made of polished wood with turned brass spokes on the wheels and places in the top for bottles. I proudly wheeled it on to the stage at rehearsals. This drinks trolley would have graced any terrace at Cannes. Michael Gover beamed. 'Perfect! Oh yes, you have done well, Rodders. Just right. Where did you find it?'

'The Co-operative Stores on . . .'

'Take it back!'

'What?'

'Take it back. The Co-op! What would my audience think if they knew I was dealing with the socialists?'

I stayed on for Pantomime. I was fascinated by the Dame. I watched him from the wings every performance, a real Lancashire, rather tired and past-it Dame. But his hands were wonderful and his feet had what ballet people call 'attitude'.

I knew that one day I'd do that, I'd play Dame, and when I did, I borrowed a lot from the Dame at Eastbourne. He sang a song and I used to sing it with him, silently in the wings, watching, learning, mouthing as he sang with great pathos, a sad song . . .

> And he's six feet three
> And he's got no swank
> And all his personality is in the bank
> TA TA TARRAH
> But I love him
> And I know that he's the one
> And I know he's clean and tidy

'Cos I bath him every Friday
And I might learn to love him
Later on! TA TA TARRAH

Then he looked at the audience and said 'Dance,' and as he did so, he began a little dance holding the corners of his pinny . . . why did he say 'dance' out loud, then do it? Why didn't he just dance? Was it the cue for the band? I dont know, but it made me smile every time.

At Stockton-on-Tees, twice nightly weekly rep (Mr Hanson did get in touch), I was walking along the street with Nicholas Brent, our camp second lead who was wearing his overcoat with the astrakhan collar. He was very animated, complaining loudly – hands flopping all over the place, beseeching the heavens . . . 'And if that dizzy cow gives me a duff cue in act three again as she has consistently done for the last four nights, I'll happily pull off those sequinned stockings of hers and wrap them around her lily-white neck . . .' He broke off in full flow. Seeing a group of theatregoers coming towards us he turned to me and said in a different voice, quieter and more baritone: 'Butch up! Fans!' Then to them in a deeper still voice, 'Hello. Did you enjoy the play?'

I moved into a room of a large Victorian house in West Hampstead My landlady Mrs Godfrey was perhaps forty something. She was a Bloomsbury lady, tall with a wonderful sense of humour and something I don't know much about called TASTE. She had an antique stall in Portobello Road and sometimes I used to drive her van for her. Why do I describe all this? Well, I was to spend quite a large chunk of my life in this flat, and Mrs Geraldine Godfrey was to become a great friend.

I can see her now. She used to talk non-stop and laugh and listen,

(*Left*) Grandma and Grandad Parkinson, my mum's parents

(*Above*) Grandma Bewes, my dad's mum

(*Below*) Me and Geoffrey, my elder brother

(*Below left*) A Yorkshireman in Luton

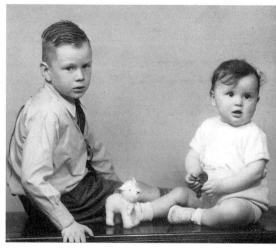

(*Left*) Rodney as
Joe the Fat Boy – early
television appearance

(*Above*) In rehearsal at
P.A.R.A.D.A.

(*Below*) 2765108 A•C•2.
Bewes, R. In the R.A.F

(*Above*) As a policeman in Watford rep

(*Below*) With my bohemian friends in Soho

(*Left*) With Tom Courtenay on the set of *Billy Liar*

(*Below*) On tour with Sir Ralph

FACING PAGE (*Above*) My favourite photo of myself

(*Below*) Jimmy and me with Wendy Richard and Wanda Ventham

Radio Times

SIXPENCE   SOUTH AND WEST EDITION

BBC
tv
Sound

THE LIKELY LADS

James Bolam and
Rodney Bewes in a new
television comedy series

FRIDAY: see page 47

Radio Times,
February and June 1965,
front covers

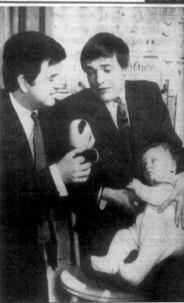

Radio Times

SIXPENCE   LONDON AND SOUTH-EAST

BBC-1
tv
BBC-2

The Likely Lads

James Bolam and Rodney Bewes are back
in another series of adventures beginning
on Wednesday on BBC-2

SEE PAGE 39

Trooping the Colour

On the Home Service and BBC-1 you can
follow the traditional parade for the
Queen's official birthday

SATURDAY

Royal Ascot

BBC-1 and the Light Programme cover this
great racing and social occasion (see page 29)

FROM TUESDAY

The Second Test

Lord's is the venue and there is coverage
on the Third Network, BBC-1, and BBC-2

FROM THURSDAY

Cooper v. Prescott

The title fight for the British and Empire
Heavyweight Championship on the Light

TUESDAY

Film in *Sportsview* on BBC-1

(*Above*) Jimmy and me
with Nerys Hughes
and Sandra Blaine

(*Below*) We all fancied
Isobel Black

(*Above left*) Jimmy and me with Bartlett
Mullins, father of the maintenance shop
(*Above right*) With Wilfred Lawson

On the
Norfolk Broads

her head on one side. She had a wicked smile, and no one could say 'How interesting' as cuttingly as GG.

I remember, I met her off the train when I was at York rep. She was looking very imposing in a white felt trilby hat with a white veil. She said, 'Hello Roddy, do you like it? It's my Max Miller look. GG was quite tall and you could hardly call her svelte. 'I've always been a big woman, Roddy,' she said. 'That's why James Robertson Justice and I were so very ridiculous in bed together. A mean lover, darling. The only pressie he ever gave me was a brace of grouse, sent from Scotland and they were high on arrival. Though he did teach me something. He told me what your navel was for. To put salt in when you are eating celery and stilton in bed with your lover. I'm not shocking you, am I?'

GG had hosts of wonderful friends. Her brother, the famous left-wing Professor JD Bernal, used to come to Sunday lunch which was always an occasion. I sat on the floor by the stove in GG's big living-room and listened to Bish Elstob, a naval commander in the war, torpedoed, then on a raft for ninety hours. He also escaped from two POW camps before being sent to Colditz Castle. He was very funny, couldn't say his 'r' sound and called me Wodney. Colditz was appawently escape-pwoof. I asked him what it was really like. 'Well Woodney, you see, everybody was there . . . George Harwood . . .'

I went for an audition at the famous Theatre Workshop at Stratford East. I wanted to get it too much. I sat in the foyer for hours, very nervous, then suddenly I was on stage. I couldn't see anyone in the auditorium, pitch black, bright lights in my face. I had been told that Gerry Raffles, Joan Littlewood's assistant, would be taking the audition, and a voice came from the darkness ahead:

'Will you sing a verse from the song "My old man said follow the van", please?'

I sang, loudly. Making up the words I didn't know, thumbs in an imaginary waistcoat. Very cockney. I sang until he stopped me.

'Thank you, thank you, now dig a hole.'

'Pardon? I've prepared . . .?'

'Just dig a hole. You know how to dig a hole, don't you?'

I dug a hole, in the middle of the stage, rolling up my sleeves and spitting on my hands, mopping my brow . . .

Then a woman's voice, gruff . . . heavy smoker? . . . deep . . . slightly off accent. Was it Joan Littlewood? 'Now will you cross the road, I mean the stage, as three different people?'

After that I had to be a runner who had just completed a four-minute mile, then, still out of breath, I had to explain to a date why I was half an hour late.

At the end of all this I said to the black void: 'Look, can you tell from this that I can act?' Naughty, but I'd had enough.

'I can see you have a very nice personality on stage.' The lady's voice again. 'Now you are a clown,' she said. 'You are a clown and someone has thrown a net over you. Like a gladiator's net thrown over a wild beast in the Coliseum, except you are a clown and not a wild beast.'

I lay spread-eagled, flat on my back, arms and legs spread out as far as they would go. I lay still like that for a minute . . . two minutes longer, three minutes . . .

Then the lady's voice again. 'Have you started?'

'Oh yes, the net's too tight, I can't move!'

'That's all. Thank you.'

'They've pegged it down into the sand and . . .'

The voice now very cross. 'Thank you and goodbye.'

I left. I didn't hear from them. I was never one of the stars of the

Theatre Workshop at Stratford East or any of their West End transfers, and now you know why.

But I was determined to work in London. I'd done rep and it had done me. I wanted to get myself on television, whatever it took.

Chapter 10

I DROVE TO SEE my parents to tell them my plan.

They gave me a transistor radio for my twenty-third birthday. I was overwhelmed. 'Oh, wasn't it far too much?'

My Dad, with such a long look, said: 'You know, Rodney, I'd give you the moon if I could.'

The next morning the telephone rang with a job. It looks like my plans are coming to fruition already. The part is the wireless operator in *Private Potter* on ATV Playhouse, and I am to be paid forty-eight pounds! It is to be screened on 6th April.

Leo McKern   Ralph Michael

James Maxwell

Brewster Mason

and

Tom Courtenay

in

PRIVATE POTTER

by Ronald Harwood and Casper Wrede

with Eric Thompson

Cast in order of appearance:

(and twenty-one names down, was)

Signals Operator . . . . Rodney Bewes

I felt I was in the major league. I was in awe of them, but enjoyed every minute.

I went to see *Billy Liar* for the third time. The stage doorman knew me by then. I bounded up the stairs and knocked on Albert Finney's door. There was a fellow feeling between us northerners. We felt we were doing something new and different in our acting. Albert was like an elder brother to us and we all looked up to him.

He took me to the Seven Stars Grill upstairs at Lyon's Corner House on Coventry Street. Roast beef, carved at the table and jacket potatoes with cream and chives. He was to leave *Billy Liar* to be in *Luther,* John Osborne's latest play. I told him about being in *Private Potter* with Tom Courtenay.

'Oh, he's taking over from me in *Billy Liar* at the Cambridge Theatre.' Tom came from Hull while Albert was from Salford. There was more than just the Pennines dividing them: Albert being big, brash and cocky, whilst Tom was into himself and quiet.

Tom had left RADA and gone straight to the Old Vic to play Constantin in *The Seagull*, and Feste in *Twelfth Night*. Now he was to be Billy Liar. I reckoned the authors would be pleased with Tom as Billy Liar, because even in Billy's fantasies he is gauche whereas I reckoned Albert's Billy could have conquered the world. Tom's Billy was never going to London to be a scriptwriter, whilst Albert's could have gone on to Hollywood.

Tom Courtenay's opening night was a great success. Fergus Cashin, in the *Daily Sketch* said: 'The audience hugged him with their chuckles.' I know that, because it was painted up outside the theatre under a big photograph of Tom, and under a big neon sign. His name in lights.

Albert opened in *Luther* at the Phoenix Theatre.

I went to see Leila Blake, who was to direct three one-act plays in a triple bill called *Counterpoint* for the Dublin Festival.

'You would be very right for Seely in the Pinter play,' she said.

'Oh, er . . . [pause] . . . really?'

'Yes. Here's the script. The Pinter play is called *A Night Out*. First in Dublin, then in the Comedy Theatre in the West End.'

When the play did transfer to the West End the mighty critic Kenneth Tynan thought the evening as a whole was doubtful but said, '. . . the acting of Rodney Bewes achieved a peak'. To this day I've never known whether it was a peak of all-time doubtfulness or a bit above, but this was my London debut and at the time I was very excited.

Tom Courtenay and I were becoming friends. I went to see him twice in *Billy Liar,* and went backstage. The stage doorman said 'To see Tom, now, eh?'

'S'right, Bob."

'You know the way.'

I knocked on the door.

'Shall we go to the pub by the front?' he said. He told me he lived in Highbury, North London, that his mother was very ill and in hospital and that he supported Hull Kingston Rovers. His run in *Billy Liar* was soon to be over, and he was to start a film. 'Directed by Tony Richardson, you know.'

'Oh, er . . . yeah.'

'*The Loneliness of the Long Distance Runner.*'

'I've read it.'

'No, when I was at University College, I never thought I should . . .'

'Oh, I never went to school much.'

'Then I went to RADA, down the road . . .'

'Oh, I was expelled from RADA.'

'What for?'

'Whoring!'

'You're a liar, you're worse than Billy.'

Tom Courtenay finished filming *The Loneliness of the Long Distance Runner* and was about to start filming *Billy Liar.* Tom's mother died in Hull. She never saw him in *The Runner,* or in *Billy Liar,* but she knew he was doing well. On Saturday nights, after two shows, Tom would take trains back to Hull to sit at her bedside for a few hours on a Sunday, and make her laugh with lines from *Billy,* doing Billy's mum.

Tom and I went to the Establishment Club which Peter Cook had opened in Greek Street. It was the place to go. Lenny Bruce was on and he was followed by Frankie Howerd, who had relaunched his career there, discovering, he said, something called 'satire'. After Lenny Bruce, whose language was, er, what's the word, well it wasn't just blue . . . Frankie started with: 'If you think I'm going to speak like that bloke you had on here last week you can all piss off.'

This night, Tom was in a strange mood. He asked me to come home with him and to stay the night. I could see he was upset, so off we went. . .

Tom's flat overlooked Highbury Fields. I was to sleep on the sofa in a big room overlooking trees and grass, with a great circular black-and-white blown-up photograph of Ellen Terry on the chimney piece. In the corners of the room stood two black pyramids containing speakers for a hi-fi system. When we arrived the flat was very crowded with visitors. I seem to remember John Thaw and Nicol Williamson there. I wondered if Tom wanted me there because he was afraid of Nicol, we all were.

Eventually, we were alone and Tom told me his mother had died. He said *The Loneliness of the Long Distance Runner* was to open the next day in London. All he could think about was how much she would have loved to have been there. He was very close to his mother and had kept all her letters. He couldn't sleep, and I don't think I did . . . but I did find something to read, when eventually I was left alone, a lovely fat screenplay in blue covers, the film script of *Billy Liar*.

I bumped into an old friend from Soho, Peter Tebbitt, at the market in Portobello Road. He was standing next to a girl.

'Who's this then?' said the refreshingly blunt northerner.

'S'me sister,' said Peter. 'Her name is Nina.'

She was very young, a natural blonde, and very sweet and unspoilt – unworldly. I could see that immediately I took her off for coffee, to where the market people went, and her brother looked worried as we left.

We talked and talked and stared at one another. The only places she had ever been were the village in Cornwall where her aunts lived in a house high up on the cliffs, an all-girls' school, and now an all-girls' college. She was nineteen and training to be a teacher. Her fair hair was cut short, she had piercing blue eyes and was wearing a blue-and-white striped top and blue cotton trousers to just below her knees. She looked like a Breton sailor-boy.

Nina and I went to Cornwall to stay at the coastguard cottages in a village between Falmouth and Penzance. She took me to see her aunts' house, high up on the cliffs, towards the Lizard, the most southerly tip of Cornwall. She knew everybody, Henry and Rene Jane who lived up the hill, the other side of the village, welcomed us with open arms. Henry had great bushy eyebrows and Rene was a jolly mother figure. We sat in her kitchen while she made pasties, real home-made pasties.

I went fishing with Henry and his friend Buller, crabbing with pots. Their boat was called *Minerva*. The fishing boats were launched down the beach in the early dawn on timbers and winched up when they came home on a winch installed in 1910. All the fishermen had nicknames; Lamby and Bunny, Jimma, Sharky and Rambo. Nina called them 'The Beastly Fishermen'.

Inside that script for the film of *Billy Liar* had been the address of the film company. Behind Tom's back, I had copied it down. Was that a terrible thing to do? I wrote to the casting director. I didn't say I was a friend of Tom's. I had a reply from Miriam Brickman, asking me to come and see her in Bruton Street in Mayfair.

Miriam Brickman was more than nice, listening patiently to my long and impressive list of credits and equally long life story. She said, 'Do you know, there's a very good part you could play in the film . . . Billy's best friend Arthur!'

'Oh, I just thought something like er . . . a little part, I didn't expect . . .'

At that moment the door opened and Tom walked into the room with John Schlesinger, who was to direct the film.

Miriam said, 'Oh hello Tom, John, this is Rodney Bewes, and I think he would be very right for Arthur.'

'Oh, hello Rodney.'

John Schlesinger beamed at me like a bearded Mr Pickwick, but Tom looked at me, the way he does, like a school prefect. I blurted out, 'Look, I didn't say I knew you. I'm not using you. I just wrote to Miriam . . . I didn't even say I read the script. I only wanted a little part, 'cos I saw Albert three times and you twice . . . I, look . . . I . . .'

Everybody laughed, and Tom said, 'Shut up, Rodney.'

'Would you like to come up on to the roof?' John said. 'I would like to film you talking to Tom.'

We followed him up on to the roof of that building in Bruton Street, high above Mayfair, and in the sunshine John filmed Tom and me talking to each other on a small hand–held Bolex camera. What did we talk about?

Well, I was staying with Tom that night, so as John said, very quietly . . .

'Ready? . . . and action.' The camera whirred.

Tom: Er, how're doing, Rodney?

Rod: Oh, grand . . . y'know.

Tom: Yeah, d'you fancy . . . er, doing anything tonight?

Rod: Like what . . . like?

Tom: Well, like going out . . . or something?

Rod: Oh, up to you . . . what do you fancy, like?

Tom: No. I wouldn't mind stopping in.

Rod: Right then, I'll do some shopping when I get out of here, I mean when I get back. D'you want some meat, I'll get steak, shall I?

Tom: Yes, steak, get some steak.

Rod: I'll get some steak.

Tom: And chips, them crinkled chips.

Rod: Right we'll have steak and chips . . .

Chapter 11

BILLY LIAR WAS filmed in Bradford. Tom was Billy, of course, and Mona Washbourne was Billy's mother. Leonard Rossiter was Billy's boss, Wilfred Pickles was his dad, and Topsy Jane was to be the main girl, Liz. Tom had been to the Royal Court to see Arnold Wesker's *Chips With Everything* and liked a boy in it, George Innes, who he thought would be right for Stamp who works with Billy and Arthur in their office.

We were staying at the Midland Hotel. I arrived on a damp Sunday evening when everyone was still out filming. I went for a walk and looked at those dark streets where I had come as a young lad for sun ray treatment with my mother – that odd smell, wearing those Biggles goggles, my little chest bare and in those 'shorts provided'.

I found a pub where I had two pints of strong Yorkshire bitter. Then I went back to the hotel and found Topsy in the lounge talking to a publicity lady, so I left them to it.

My first day, and at breakfast Topsy thought it funny for me to be so nervous, in my new suit and make-up at seven o'clock in the morning.

Topsy Jane had also been in *The Loneliness of the Long Distance*

Runner with Tom with another promising newcomer, James Bolam. Topsy was from Birmingham and was a nice girl–next–door without pretensions to being a filmstar.

Tom and I rehearse, and I find the crowds very off-putting. John Schlesinger couldn't have been nicer and kinder. He whispered in my ear, when everyone else was fraught and shouting and impatient. 'Take your time, Rodney, take your time. Don't let them rush you. We can always do it again.'

We were filming this difficult tracking shot up an incline, the big Panavision camera pulled up tracks on ropes. The shot took hours to set up, then Tom and I had to keep the exact distance from the camera for the focus, which was very tight. The lighting cameraman, Denys Coop, was worried about the clouds, the operator Jack Atchelor was worried about the track, the sound men were worried about the spectators and I was worried about everything. John Schlesinger remained patient and calm.

Frank Ernst (first assistant director): 'Quiet! Please! Can we have no more noise QUIET! Turn over!'
('Turn over' means switch on the camera.)
Jack shouts: 'RUNNING!'
Peter (sound) shouts: 'SPEED!'
The tape machine is running, 'beep beep' goes the indicator it's at speed.
Frank: 'MARK IT!'
I'm looking at Pamela Mann, continuity, to see she's got her finger on the right bit of the script with the lines in it.
The clapper loader shouts: 'SCENE SEVENTY TWO! TAKE ONE!' and claps his board shut, just missing my nose, and John Schlesinger, very quietly, says 'Action!'

Tom and I begin to follow the camera up the track. We are two old Yorkshire councillors talking made-up 'councillor speak'.

'Ee I'm fair clemmed, mysen.'

'Aye lad I'm fair thraiped.'

And to an imaginary passer-by, 'Na then, Ernest, ow is ter?'

'There's allus bin an Olroyd at Olroyd's mill and ther allus will be!'

I felt it was going quite well and even began to enjoy myself when a man ducked under the ropes keeping the crowds back, and stepped right between Tom and me and the camera. 'CUT IT!'

'No, just a minute, I knew your father, Horace, Horace Bewes, wasn't it? Electricity showrooms, Bradford!'

It took hours to set up the shot again. We all went back to the hotel. John was very nice and made everybody laugh about it, but I didn't feel it was all that funny.

Tom and I went out that evening. Two Yorkshire lads. We went to a pub where there was a piano player who played songs Tom's mother used to play and Tom had tears in his eyes. He gave the piano player a pound.

Some lunchtimes Tom and I went off to play snooker above Burton's Tailoring. When an assistant director came to get us he told me off for not being back on the location. 'Dear me Rodney, for heaven's sake, everyone's waiting. You knew what time we were starting again!' And this in front of everyone. Then he turned to Tom. 'All right Tommy, love? Did you get a bite of lunch?'

It takes two to play snooker, I thought.

On location I sat in a caravan provided for Tom to relax in between takes. He was interviewed by a lady from the *Daily Herald*.

I couldn't help listening. He was talking about playing Hamlet and Hollywood film offers.

Sometimes Tom just wanted to sit quietly with his script, and I crept away. He was concentrating. Billy is a big, complicated part and Tom was very serious, but he could do it. After all, at grammar school in Hull, Tom had won the 'Amy Johnson Memorial Prize for GRIT'.

One night, he treated me to dinner and John Schlesinger bought the wine, Mouton Cadet Rothschild 1955. I started with *pâté maison* with a bit of lettuce out of which crawled a slug! I said, 'Probably trying to get into pictures.' – Which everyone thought funny. Then I took a cigar from the waiter with the box and no one seemed to think it was out of the ordinary. Ee, Rods . . .

A terrible thing happened while filming *Billy Liar*. Topsy Jane became ill. I loved Topsy. She was a happy uncomplicated Birmingham girl. I can see her now, pouting lips and a big sad sigh. 'Ooh, Rodney, all this show business isn't me, I'd just luv to have kids, you know. I'd luv to work in a nursery, that's what I'd really like.'

I saw the first signs of her illness when John Schlesinger asked me if I would go to see the 'daily rushes'. I told John I didn't really like going to rushes, but he said, 'I want you to come, Rodney.'

And that was good enough for me. Up on the huge wide screen at the cinema, I stared at the scenes, not just yesterday's work but some earlier takes that John wanted me to see too. They were Topsy's scenes, and something was very wrong. She said the lines but nothing was coming from Topsy. It was like watching a zombie.

John looked at me when the lights went up. 'Do you see it?'

'Yes.'

'Do you know what's wrong?'

'No.'

'Is she unhappy about anything?'

'I don't know.'

He said: 'Rodney, I want you to take her out, to the cinema, for a meal, will you? Try to see if you can cheer her up. See if you can do something, anything.'

I don't know if they had talked to Tom. He had a lot on, playing the lead. Perhaps they didn't want to upset him? It upset me.

Topsy and I went to the pictures, and I remember thinking it odd she insisted on sitting in the front row, too near the noisy screen. It was a cowboy film. We sat in the middle of the row, and Topsy didn't stop eating sweets, staring up at the screen like a child on her best behaviour, being good, silent, and nothing coming out of her. Then we went for a meal and if there was something wrong, she didn't confide in me.

Nina came up for a couple of nights and we had a meal in the Midland, with Topsy. Still no clues, as we all wondered what 'Pamplemouse Cerisette' was, and ordered 'Ris de Veau Bonne-Maman' at 17/6d, 'Saumon Froid Mayonnaise' three shillings extra, and 'Glacé Divers' to follow.

The next morning John was getting into a car outside the hotel: 'Get in, Rodney. Come and scout locations with me.'

'I'm sorry, I seem to have failed with Topsy.'

'I'm going to see the big Mecca ballroom for the dance hall scenes.'

The manager was sent for, a big fat man with waistcoat and moustache.

'Oh hello, my name is John Schlesinger and I'm in Bradford shooting an important feature film. Now, we need a dance hall for, oh, three or four days . . .'

'You don't want this one?'

'Er, yes, possibly, if. . .'

'Get away! You couldn't afford it. There's thirty-seven thousand light bulbs in that ceiling alone!'

So the whole unit moved to Ashton-under-Lyme, near Manchester, to the Ashton Palais, Gas Street.

I was sorry to leave Bradford and my cosy room at the Midland. In the foyer, watching the unit leaving, I was talking to the head porter, by the doors as we watched Wilfred Pickles carry his bags from the lift to the waiting car. He repeated the journey, oh, three or four times, bringing down his suitcases and carrying them out. Wilfred was very well known for his radio show *Have a Go*, and his catchphrase, 'Give 'em the money, Mabel'.

Now, watching him carry his things through the marble hall of the Midland's grand foyer, the porter said to me with great dignity: 'We honestly do not mind if he gives us a tip or not Rodney, but to have to stand here and watch Wilfred Pickles carry his own bags out to car . . . well, it's terrible, isn't it?'

I went back up to my room and rang down to the desk. 'Send a porter up for my bags, er . . . bag, will you? Straight away please, room 62.' And when we passed the head porter in the foyer, his face broke into the biggest grin. 'Goodbye, Mr Bewes.'

Ashton is part of the bronchial belt of Manchester. You can hear the people coughing as far away as Blackpool. The young boys and girls whose dance hall this was did wonderful formal dances across the floor, like a sort of Sixties line dance, arms linked, all in time. The girls were dressed up in figure-hugging skirts and dresses and our technicians' eyes were popping out of their heads, staring at their tight bums.

But at Ashton, that week in November, the fun went out of it all because I learned that Topsy was going home and her part was to be recast. Poor, dear Topsy. She had something called schizophrenia simplex and it was incurable.

Julie Christie got the part, and John Schlesinger reshot Liz's scenes in Bradford, and to save time, he came up with this montage of shots, the camera sweeping through the streets, and Julie swinging her shoulder bag along the pavement. It turned out to be more than just a sequence to save time. It gave Julie Christie a swinging entrée to movies.

Nina and I went to Cornwall that spring, and I marvelled at the village in May, all the wild flowers in the hedgerows and the wonderful walks. At night we sat by the fire and could hear the sea. Nina told me that when we first met: 'I was so very flattered you even noticed me.'

We got engaged.

Chapter 12

OUR WEDDING-DAY was set for 10th August.
Tom Courtenay said he'd be the best man, so we decided to have 'Jerusalem' from *The Loneliness of the Long Distance Runner* for him and for Topsy.

Then Tom backed out. To this day I don't know why. So I asked my friend Roy Battersby. It was too late to change the hymns, so 'Jerusalem' was still in, and 'All Things Bright and Beautiful'.

I didn't have a stag night, just went to dinner at Nina's parents' house in Mill Hill village, Nina's brother brought a friend, a Jewish friend, Peter Rand, a fashion photographer. Nina's father did the cooking: fillet steak and flageolet beans and lovely St Emilion wine. I felt very strange about getting married in the morning and Nina was nervous too.

Nina's Papa went on and on about Jews. He called them stinking Yids! Meanwhile Peter Rand was just sitting there with a gentle smile on his face.

Suddenly, I could bear it no longer. I got up mid-bite and left the room. In the billiard room I set the balls up. Then Nina's brother burst in, obviously upset. 'How dare you be so rude, just leaving the table like that! You treat this house like . . . to just leave your food

. . . My father . . .' He aimed a great swing at me . . . and it connected. Right square on the jaw, and down I went. I fell with a billiard cue in my hand, all the time thinking what a great weapon it was. But I hauled myself up, put the cue back on the table and left the house. I climbed into my little van, and drove back home. I wasn't thinking about much at all, certainly not about poor Nina. I was just imagining the scene in the dining-room.

'He's gone.'

'What do you mean gone?'

'Gone where?'

'I don't know. I hit him!'

'Oh God.'

'Is he coming back, do you think?'

Was Nina wondering if I was going to return?

Perhaps Papa was hoping I wouldn't?

I took the phone off the hook, went to bed and slept like a top.

The next morning I was trying to collect my thoughts. What was I getting married for? The same reasons I went off to do National Service? To be normal? At the Tavistock Clinic, Dr Israel had said I could get out of National Service because I was seeing him, but I had wanted to be normal, respectable. Nina was certainly that. She was so different to my weirdy friends.

Nina looked pleased to see me at the end of the aisle, but while everybody was singing 'All Things Bright and Beautiful' I was thinking, 'What am I doing?'

Nina told me afterwards I had been a strange hue of grey-green. Well, I had had a lot of St Emilion the night before.

The wedding night, oh dear! I'd bought a great brass bed; it was all in bits on the floor of our new flat. Nina, my child bride, and I tried to put it together, but it kept falling down, so we gave up and slept on the mattress on the floor.

We didn't go away on honeymoon, because *Billy Liar* was opening at the Warner West End in Leicester Square. Dilys Powell from the *Sunday Times* said:

> For a moment I wondered whether the actor himself, Tom Courtenay, lacked the precise edge of comedy needed . . . the performance is an astonishing development of the performance he gave in the London stage production. . . . Rodney Bewes brings good comic timing to his role as Billy's friend.

Thank you Dilys, and thank you Philip Oakes in the *Sunday Telegraph*:

> There is a beautifully dogged sketch of a reluctant wage-slave by Rodney Bewes. And – as Billy's free-wheeling girlfriend – Julie Christie is full to the brim with juice and joy.
>
> There is also Tom Courtenay, whose playing here deserves at least a dozen Oscars. Along with Alan Bates, Albert Finney, and Richard Harris, he is amongst the very best of the current crop of young English actors.

A sad letter arrived from my Dad. Through his connections in local goverment he had arranged for my brother to move to a council house. The letter was typed, and from his office. I expect he'd drafted it quite a few times. He was a dear man and it must have pained him.

Tel. Luton 53222.Ext.21

Eastern Electricity Board
487, Dunstable Road
Luton, Beds.
22nd August 1963

I don't know how to start as I have never been in this position before. Geoffrey has landed me in the cart. A few weeks ago, he had the bailiffs in for arrears of rent (over £24) and I cleared that for him. Since then I have lent him another £26 making a total of £50.

The trouble is I borrowed money hoping that he would pay me back, which he promised, by the end of this month, but he has not paid back anything at all. I am trusting you both to keep this from Mum as I would do anything to avoid hurting or upsetting her.

I sent him the money and said I hadn't told Nina and that it would be our secret.

Nina was teaching at a school in Hendon. We weren't really seeing much of each other. In the evenings she was tired or preparing work.

One day during rehearsals for a play for ITV called *Loop*, the whole of ATV seemed to be in a great state of excitement. What was it? As I walked down the long corridor to the canteen, there was a definite buzz about the place, and as I went past one of the big studio doors, I bumped into Eric Morecambe: 'Steady, young man, who's after you? Is it Lew? I saw you in a very good play on the telly.'

Oh my . . . Eric Morecambe knows me! 'Oh, huh, yeah, what's all the . . .? D'you know what's happening? S'like the Queen's coming. She's not, is she?'

'Come with me, young man!'

Eric Morecambe took me into the big studio where they were rehearsing for the *Morecambe and Wise Show*. Long tiers of seats facing the stages. I hadn't seen studio audience seating before. In the seats were groups of people from the other studios and on the studio floor, groups of people from the canteen, from the offices . . . cleaning ladies . . . guards from the main gates . . .

'There you go, that's what it's all about!' He pointed out four lads, three with guitars and a drummer, rather smart in suits. On the drum it said The Beatles.

I said: 'Well, they'll never get on with a name like that, beetles!'

But when they launched into 'SHE LOVES YOU . . . SHE LOVES YOU, YEAH YEAH YEAH,' wow, the whole place went up, and I knew what the buzz was about.

I kept an appointment in November to go and see a director friend at ATV. We went to the Red Lion at Elstree where the people from the film studios across the road used to come and have a drink after filming. I sat on a high stool at the bar, and got talking to the guy on the stool on the other side of me, a big American with sleepy eyes, very laid back and slowly I began to realise it was Robert Mitchum . . . those droopy, heavy-lidded eyes. As we were talking, a little Irish chap comes up and sticks his nose into Robert Mitchum's face.

'Ah, so's you're the big man, eh? Well take that . . .' and he swung a punch and missed. Mitchum got off his stool slowly and very gently held the Irishman at arm's length. The little fellow's punches couldn't reach and he looked very funny throwing punches into the air. After a while his mates took him away.

'Does that happen a lot?' I asked,

'Sure . . . they wanna go home and tell the missus they took a swing at Robert Mitchum.'

'What? Like "I'm home, dear, guess who I laid out tonight in the pub? Robert Mitchum!" "That's right dear, your dinner's in the oven, a nice piece of haddock!"'

He said: 'I saw you in that er . . . science fiction play on television.'

Oh Lord, Robert Mitchum has seen me in a television play, and then someone came into the pub and in a loud voice said:

'Kennedy's been shot! President Kennedy, he's been shot . . . dead.'

I remember Robert Mitchum's face crumbled, and there were tears in his eyes. He gave me a sad half-smile and left without a word.

I drove home. Nina was tired from a day at school.

I had got the part in *A Midsummer Night's Dream* of Flute, one of the 'rude mechanicals' who with Bottom (Sir Ralph Richardson) put on the play within the play, for the court of Athens. Rehearsals began and I had lots of ideas for Flute, who has of course to dress up as a woman for his part of Thisbe. Lots of actors do Flute as being all embarrassed at having to play a woman. I thought my Flute would be proud to. Embarrassed, sure, but what an honour to do a play before the Duke of Athens and all his court . . . yes . . . humble too, and sincere, but most of all proud to do his part well in front of the gentry.

At one point in the play poor Thisbe comes on to find her love quite dead across the stage, his wooden sword stuck firmly in his upstage armpit . . . well you hoped to find the sword there, but with Sir Ralph you couldn't be too sure. He also liked to try something new now and again.

We were rehearsing on stage and Sir Ralph as Bottom had died a long death upon his wooden sword and Rodney, alias Flute alias Thisbe, enters and stands over her lover's corpse in front of the Duke of Athens, his fair Hippolyta and all the court.

(ENTER Flute AS Thisbe)

THESEUS: Here she comes and her passion ends the play.
FLUTE: Asleep, my love?

> What, dead, my dove?
> Speak, speak. Quite dumb?
> Dead, dead? A tomb
> Must cover thy sweet eyes.
> These lily lips,
> This cherry nose,
> These yellow cowslip cheeks
> Are gone, are gone.
> Lovers make moan.
> His eyes were green as leeks.

I was sincere, heart-broken about my lost love but also *proud* of showing the court what good acting was all about! Anyway, when I got to . . .

> These lily lips,
> This cherry nose,
> These yellow cowslip cheeks . . .

Sir Ralph sat up . . . 'Hey, hey, Ah have an idea! If you play with me lily lips, me nose and me cheeks, boy, it'll get a big laugh, eh? You see, ah'm supposed to be dead and . . .'

I said, 'I don't want to do that.'

There was a long and terrible silence until our lovely director, Wendy Toye said: 'Well, I do think we must get on, and Rodney must speak to Sir Ralph afterwards.'

And so we went on.

But after rehearsal, I had to go and see Sir Ralph, up a long corridor to the number one dressing-room at the Queen's Theatre. I knocked. 'Enter,' and there was the great man slumped in an armchair . . . I was frightened. He looked up and said, very kindly, 'Why don't you want to play with my face, boy? Ah think it would be funny. Ah've done a lot of comedy . . . ah do think ah know a little bit about it . . . ?'

I took a deep breath. 'You come on as Bottom, well, Pyramus, and before the whole Court, you have this marvellous speech, a whole page in Temple's Shakespeare, and then I come on, and I have this great speech, a whole page in Temple's and er . . . I don't want to share it with you.'

Another long and terrible pause.

'Oh, ah see . . . well . . .' he said, decisively, if you do it well, you won't have to play with my face, but if you do it *badly* . . .'

And here he just nodded his head. His patient, kind look was telling me the interview was over and that I was all right if I did it well.

A few days later I was parking my Rolls, of which I was extremely proud, behind the Queen's Theatre, and Sir Ralph rode up and parked his beloved BMW motorbike nearby. He walked round to me, pulling off his big gauntlet gloves and sweeping dust from his brogues with them. 'Is she yours, boy? What year is she?'

'Oh yes, Sir Ralph, 1937.'

Then absentmindedly, 'Ah wouldn't mind a spin . . . one day?'

'Oh, any time, Sir Ralph, I would be thrilled!'

Perhaps he did it to show that after our little talk the other day, there was no animosity between us, no bad feelings. He always treated me with kindly amused slight disbelief and I near worshipped him.

'Well, boy, what about tomorrow? Lunch at the Athenaeum . . . Hmm?'

'Oh yes . . . right, tomorrow then . . . right.'

I was up early the next day, shaved carefully, dressed carefully and with my bucket and shammy leather, oh, I cleaned that car and polished it. Then after the morning's rehearsal in my suit and a tie, I wondered if he had remembered.

'Ready, boy? Hey, hey? Got enough . . . er gas?'

'Oh yes, Sir Ralph.' And I helped him into the Rolls.

'Ah should be sitting in the back. Oh, ha, ha, ah'm such a wag!'

I drove off very carefully, double-clutching beautifully, down Shaftesbury Avenue and around Piccadilly Circus to Pall Mall, and the grand stucco columns of the Athenaeum Club full of bishops and heads of state. I pulled on the handbrake beside the driver's door, leapt out and around to help my famous passenger out.

'Thank you, thank you, lovely fun . . . you drive her very well, I'll only be fifty-five minutes, perhaps just an hour. Will you take me back too?'

I had thought I was going to lunch at the Athenaeum! 'Oh yes, of course . . . I'll wait . . . Ha.'

And Sir Ralph lifted his hat, a brown trilby, and waved it as he entered the grand portals. 'Hey hey, fifty-five minutes then . . . not more than an hour.'

While we were rehearsing another strange and inexplicable thing happened. Wendy Toye asked Alan Howard, Julian Glover and myself for a drink in the White Horse, across from the stage door. 'I would like to see Alan and Julian and Rodney, when rehearsal is over, *for a little chat.*'

Curious? I thought, what have I done now?

'Now, the reason I have asked you here . . . well, there are six very young girls in the company. Six dancers from the Royal Ballet. My fairies: Peaseblossom, Cobweb, Mustardseed and well, I am personally responsible to Dame Ninette de Valois for them. As far as I know, they are leaving on tour . . . intact! I want them to return . . . intact, if you follow.'

Why? Why we three? 'Wendy,' I said, 'there are forty men in the company.'

'I know it'll be you three!'

Should one take it as a compliment? And wasn't it a bit tough on the others?

Sir Ralph always made an entrance at rehearsals. Once he strode on to the stage and announced in a sad voice that could be heard at the back of the stalls, 'Has anyone found a talent? . . . I used to have one . . . but ah've lost it! I went to the lost luggage office at Paddington Station and asked the man in charge . . . have ya found a talent? Oh, only a little one . . . and he shook his head . . . ah have lost one, you see . . . in a silver box. A small silver box . . . no? . . . With RR on the top? No? Hey hey.'

There were many variations of this speech. One day when it was just the two of us in his dressing-room I asked him, really for want of something to say: 'Why Paddington, er . . . ?'

And he gave me a hooded look as if to say, 'Be careful boy' . . . then he said, 'Goes west . . .'

The first night at the Theatre Royal, Brighton, went very quickly, and when we got to my entrance I was quite scared. I had a lot to prove to Sir Ralph as well as the audience . . . but I did do it well, sincere, still broken-hearted Thisbe over the poor corpse of her love.

>Asleep, my love?
>What, dead, my dove?
>Speak, speak.

Here I shook my head, pathetic, sad, from side to side.

>Quite dumb?
>Dead, dead? A tomb
>Must cover thy sweet eyes.

Here goes, I thought, 'If you do it well . . . ?'

>These lily lips,
>This cherry nose,
>These yellow cowslip cheeks . . .

He hasn't moved, I thought . . . I'm winning.

>Are gone, are gone.
>Lovers make moan.
>His eyes were . . .

But now Sir Ralph whispered in a voice that could be heard in Worthing. 'Very good, boy. Very good! . . . Watch the consonants!' Well, I didn't know what he meant, but I knew he was trying to get me, and thought you won't succeed, mate.

> . . . green as leeks.
> O sisters three
> Come, come to me
> With hands as pale as milk.
> Lay them in gore.
> Since you have shore
> With shears his thread of silk.
> Tongue, not a word.
> Come, trusty sword

Sir Ralph stirred. Was he thinking of giving me the sword? I grabbed it before he could.

There was no more talk about having to play with Sir Ralph's face in my speech after that. In fact, he was kind to me. I think he liked me for my honesty and daring.

During the last week a terrible thing happened. I shall never forget it. Dear old Flute and his mates, 'the rude mechanicals', are in the forest, rehearsing their play before 'Bully Bottom' is translated into an ass. We are waiting impatiently for Bottom to come and tell us we are to do our play before the entire court of Athens, Flute muses on the possible financial rewards of playing before royalty.

FLUTE: If he come not, then the play is marred.
           It goes not forward, doth it? Oh sweet bully
           Bottom! Thus hath he lost sixpence a day during
           his life. He could not have 'scaped sixpence a day.
           And the Duke had not given him sixpence a day
           for playing Pyramus, I'll be hanged. He would
           have deserved it. Sixpence a day in Pyramus, or
           nothing,

When something goes wrong in a play, it all happens very quickly except for the poor actor involved. For him it takes a lifetime. My first clue was people darting about in the wings and loud whispers, then I saw Wendy Toye in the middle of the stalls get up and begin to edge her way to the aisle.

'Excuse me.'

'Sorry.'

'SSssssssh!'

I saw her come through the pass door to the prompt corner as I got to '. . . Sixpence a day in Pyramus, or nothing.' This was Bottom's cue. Then as nothing happened, I thought I'll throw in another . . . 'Aye, sixpence a day or nothing!'

And that's just what happened . . . nothing. I picture the script: 'ENTER BOTTOM'. He didn't The other actors looked blank, so I repeated Bottom's cue again. Nothing. Right, I thought, so that's how it is. I'm not having it.

FLUTE: Or ninepence, eh? Ninepence a day for our labours . . . Eh, lads? [Not one of them looked as if they wanted to say anything, so I thought, right, I'll try a shilling.] A shilling? To play our pieces afore the Duke? A shilling . . . One and threepence?

Well, I got up to 1/9d in threepenny bits and began to think, I'm all alone here. I decided I wasn't putting up with it. Now if you go over to someone on the stage and open your arms, sort of baring your chest and asking them a question, they've got to say something. So I went over to Quince.

FLUTE: And pray, where is dear old bully Bottom now, eh?

QUINCE: Oh, ah, er . . . I expect he's still in the er . . . forest with . . . er . . . that thing on his head!

I looked to the wings. Was Sir Ralph ill? . . . or worse?

FLUTE: Oh lads. Oh hearts, two shillings a day!
              For our travail . . . what doest think, mates?
              TWO AND THREEPENCE?

And then . . . the curtain slowly came down. I ran off the stage and through the archway and up the corridor to the number one dressing-room. When something like this happens on stage you carry with you a sort of white electricity, adrenaline mixed with blind terror. I kicked open the door. 'Where the . . . where . . .?'

I couldn't say any more. Before me was the most extraordinary sight. Sir Ralph on his back on the sofa in full armour. Complete with wooden sword. Yes, he had entirely forgotten our scene in the forest and got ready for the final scene.

I just stood looking at him with my mouth open.

'Oh, oh, boy! . . . I heard you on the Tannoy! Oh, oh, deah, you were masterful. Ah couldn't change back, I couldn't. Then when you got to . . . one and ninepence . . . from sixpence! And at one and ninepence Quince said (he was laughing so much, there were tears rolling down his cheeks), "I expect he's still in the forest . . ." oh, oh . . . "with that thing on his head!" Ah, ah, must see ah couldn't . . . Ah couldn't . . . s'only a little scene? And then you went on to two shillings! Two and threepence . . .!'

Well, I couldn't be angry, could I?

And Sir Ralph never called me 'boy' again. The next time we met, 'Hello Starry . . . hey, hey?'

Our tour was international. Mexico City, Caracas, Bogota, Quito, Lima, Santiago, Buenos Aires, Montevideo, Sao Paulo, Rio de Janeiro. Oh, and then a little trip round Europe to Lisbon, Madrid, Paris, Athens and Rome . . . no wonder Wendy Toye was warned for Dame Ninette de Valois' fairies.

In Mexico City I read in a newspaper that Alberto Finney was in Acapulco. So I thought, I'll give him a ring. Just like that.

'Er, Alberto Finney, er . . . es. La?'

'Ello?'

'Alberto Finney, actore con cinemato.'

'Aaaah Alberto Finney!'

'Yes, yes is he there?'

'No, is not ere.'

'Aaah, oh.'

'Is at Las Brisas . . . other 'otel.'

'Si, si.'

Back to directory enquiries, then,

'Si, Las Brisas.'

'Por favor? Alberto Finney?'

'One moment, please.'

Then that unmistakable Salford accent.

'Ullo?'

'Hello Albert. It's Rodney!'

'Hello kidda.'

'I'm in Mexico City.'

'S'not that far . . . d'yer wanna come over?'

Albert met me at Acapulco airport looking all tanned and healthy. He had a jeep in which he drove me to his hotel.

We sat on his terrace, high up like an eyrie, looking out over the fantastic Bay of Acapulco. It took my breath away. Then back in the jeep and down, down the zigzag road, past the other haciendas and through the gates and down to the town, where a boatman was waiting to take us scuba-diving, then waterskiing.

Albert had become a millionaire from the film of *Tom Jones*. Offered the choice of wages or percentage, he had chosen a percentage of the profits. Susannah York, who was lovely in *Tom Jones*, had been given the same choice, and lost out. Albert said, 'I didn't reckon it really, Rodney. I honestly thought of it as Tony Richardson wanking through Dorset, but I've always liked a gamble . . . so I said I'll take a percentage, and the film did big throughout the whole . . . world. China, Italy, you name it. S'a mystery to me!'

In the evening we sat on the terrace, both dressed up for an evening out, champagne on a stand in a bucket of ice. Albert had his guitar on his lap, just playing with it chords and snatches of classical Spanish pieces he was learning . . . me sipping from my glass. Out there across that famous bay, the sun like a great red orb sank into the sea, and I couldn't help myself, I cried . . . great tears rolling down my face.

'Eh, what's up?'

'Sorry, I'm sorry, can't help it . . . it's just . . . just . . .'

'I know.'

When I flew back to play *A Midsummer Night's Dream* in the theatre, Alan Howard asked me: 'And where did you get to?'

I hadn't told anyone I was going. I would never have been given permission. 'Oh, I just flew over to Acapulco, know someone who was stopping there, like, Albert Finney actually . . . we went scuba-diving and waterskiing!'

'Oh yes? Pull the other one, it's got bells on. You live in a fantasy world, you!'

The embassy receptions were hard on Sir Ralph. He couldn't appear unmannerly and took his duties as leader of the company very seriously.

He had tricks to avoid bores. He'd get tired and appeared dottier than he was. When there were just the two of us in his dressing-room, he could be very sharp, but three or four of the others came in and then his vagueness would take over.

But in Ecuador, after yet another first night, very late in the embassy garden, I was to witness something I thought I'd never see. Sir Ralph was in the shade, quite a way from the house, alone, he thought, sitting on the edge of a great cistern, a drink in his hand. He was miles away in a contented dream, his hand in the water, watching the fish swim. He didn't know – how could he? – that I was in a nearby rhododendron bush with a breathless fairy on loan from the Royal Ballet.

Then suddenly from nowhere came a pompous embassy first secretary who said, very brusquely, I thought, 'Sir Ralph, your ambassador is waiting to serve supper.'

Sir Ralph looked up and fixed the wretched man with those extraordinary eyes: 'Oh, tell our ambassador to go and fuck himself!' Shocked, the man fled.

The next day at the theatre up in the chorus dressing-room, the door was open, and there was Sir Ralph on a little wooden chair, surrounded by the dancers and quite a few of the others, all sitting around him on the floor as if he had called them together. 'And ah said to him, ah told him . . . tell our ambassador to go and fuck himself!'

He was proudly telling everyone like a naughty schoolboy who had been cheeky to a prefect. He told everyone, though I don't suppose he told Lady Richardson, our Fairy Queen, who would not have approved.

Athens was the only time I saw Sir Ralph really upset. Someone had failed to notify him about an official lunch. Sir Ralph's absence was noted in the Greek press, and it made him very angry that someone else's incompetence made him appear unmannerly. Unfair too, as so many times he had held the flag and waved it, at late night do's that weren't much fun for him.

Generally, though, we were sold out and a great success, wherever we went. I had had a great time. I had seen the volcanoes Cotopaxi and Chimborazo, swam from the beaches of Acapulco and Copacabana and played five capital cities of Europe.

At Heathrow, it was goodbye to the fairies that Dame Ninette de Valois had entrusted to Wendy Toye. 'They are leaving these shores intact and I want them to return intact,' she had said.
Well, Wendy, I can tell you now, fifty per cent of them did.

Chapter 13

THAT SUMMER OF 1964, I went to the BBC Television Centre to meet someone called Dick Clement. On the desk there was a pile of scripts, by Dick Clement and Ian La Frenais, both names new to me. It was a situation comedy series called *The Likely Lads*, about two working-class lads called Bob and Terry. 'We're thinking about James Bolam for Terry,' Dick said. 'D'you know him?'

'A bit, I've seen him around . . . like, yeah.'

'We liked *Billy Liar* . . . we want this to be real.'

'Oh, right. I can do real . . . ha!'

The scripts were terrific, but I was scared – a comedy series on television? I had done such good stuff with good writers and directors over the last two, three years. I thought I must speak to Jimmy Bolam. I'll just ring him, why not?

'What do you think of the scripts?' I said.

'They're wonderful, aren't they?'

'Yeah! Any actor would be a fool not to want to play those parts.'

Dick and Ian had met in the Uxbridge Arms, Notting Hill, London in 1961. There's a blue plaque outside to prove it -- well there should be! Ian was in something called 'market research', while Dick was in radio at the BBC's Bush House. They met. They got on. They began to write sketches together.

Ask Ian how he started as a writer and he'll say, 'Oh, we went to a pub in the Brompton Road and wrote a sketch.' Was it based on a conversation between two girls he had overheard on a bus? So legend has it. In fact the sketch was about two boys and two girls, who were discussing their success or lack of it, on a recent double date. It was performed in the revue the Ariel Players – the BBC amateur theatrical group – put on that Christmas.

BOB:	It was all right wasn't it?
TERRY:	Oh yeah.
BOB:	It was all right
TERRY:	Yeah. How d'you get on then?
BOB:	Oh, all right you know . . . you didn't seem to be doing too badly?
TERRY:	Oh well, she's all right. Deirdre. You know, I mean . . . She's all right.
BOB:	She's all right.
(PAUSE)	
TERRY:	Did you score?
BOB:	Come off it! Standing there next to a milk machine, did I score? Who do you think I am, Mighty Mouse?
TERRY:	You didn't then?
BOB:	Well, did you?
TERRY:	What, oh well, you know.
BOB:	Yeah . . . still, she was all right, mate.
TERRY:	Oh yeah.

(CUT TO THE TWO GIRLS USING BLACKOUT, LIGHTS UP TECHNIQUE TO INTER-CUT)

PAT: It was quite nice, wasn't it?

DEIRDRE: Oh yeah, it was quite nice.

PAT: Did he try anything, mine did?

DEIRDRE: I don't see how, standing in front of that milk machine.

PAT: He didn't then?

DEIRDRE: I didn't say he didn't

PAT: It was a nice night though.

DEIRDRE: Oh yeah, it was a nice night.

(LIGHTS UP ON THE BOYS)

TERRY: They were all right after a couple of drinks, though, weren't they?

BOB: Yeah, mine was drinking Babycham. What did yours have, lager?

TERRY: Yeah, but later on I got her on to Tia Maria.

BOB: Oh, are they strong like?

TERRY: Strong? A couple of those, mate, and you'd be standing in a bucket of sand singing 'The Desert Song'.

(CUT TO THE GIRLS)

PAT: You know, that taxi must have cost something.

DEIRDRE: Oh, they didn't seem to mind how much they spent – I will say that for them.

PAT: And that Chinese restaurant isn't cheap.

DEIRDRE: Oh no, no, no, I will say that for them.

PAT: They didn't seem to mind *how* much they spent.

DEIRDRE: No, they didn't seem to mind what we had.

(CUT TO THE LADS)

TERRY: I haven't half spent some bloody money tonight!

BOB: I must have spent nearly two quid.

TERRY: I spent three.

BOB: Well, you would get that taxi.

TERRY: Oh well, you know.

BOB: What's the matter with the bus?

TERRY: Oh well, you know.

BOB: Eh, I've nearly spent three, too. I got that last round.

TERRY: In that cocktail lounge, no draught beer and two bob for a Double Diamond.

(CUT TO THE GIRLS)

PAT: Deirdre . . . you know that Bob?

DEIRDRE: Yeah.

PAT: Well, he kisses with his mouth open.

DEIRDRE: Well?

PAT: Do you?

DEIRDRE: Well, yeah.

PAT: No, but I mean not just like that. (SHE OPENS HER MOUTH A LITTLE) But wide, like that. (SHE OPENS HER MOUTH WIDE, Deirdre FOLLOWS SUIT)

DEIRDRE: Like that?

PAT: Um, like that!

DEIRDRE: No, I don't, not like that.

PAT: Well, he does. (SHE OPENS HER MOUTH VERY WIDE) Like THAT!

DEIRDRE: It's a wonder he doesn't bloody choke himself.

PAT: Want a fag?

DEIRDRE: No thanks.

PAT: D'you think they'll ask us out again?

DEIRDRE: Oh, I don't know, they might. He seemed quite keen on you.

PAT: Do you think so? Do you know he gave me all his luncheon vouchers for next week?

DEIRDRE: Did he?

PAT: Yeah, ever so nice of him.

DEIRDRE: Um, yes.

(CUT TO THE LADS)

TERRY: You gave her all your luncheon vouchers?

BOB: Oh well, you know.

TERRY: What's the matter with you, are you some kind of a nut? What are you going to live on all next week?

BOB: Oh well, you know . . . do you reckon you'll see her again?

TERRY: Maybe, maybe not. What about you then?

BOB: Oh, I dunno.

TERRY: (TEASING HIM) Eh!

BOB: I dunno!

TERRY: Eh!

BOB: Oh, get on with ya.

TERRY: Aye, cheerio then, mate.

BOB: Yeah, cheerio.

TERRY: See ya.

BOB: Yeah, you know what, though?

TERRY: What?

BOB: She's all right

TERRY: Oh yeah.

THE END

Nowadys that sketch might seem a bit tame, but in those pre-Pill days of the early Sixties it was realistic, funny, even daring.

Later Dick was sent on the BBC's television director's course, which ended with each trainee making a short exam piece with a budget of £100, which was then put on to film and shown to those on high at the BBC. Dick got out and dusted 'Double Date' and four actors were cast in the roles. Laurie Asprey was Terry and Brian Miller was Bob, the girls were Coral Atkins and Valerie Varnham.

To save money, Dick hit on the idea of a stills photomontage for 'The Date', a device he later was to use very successfully, as it added speed and was good visually. They went to a pub and a Wimpy Bar to take the photographs. The rehearsal and recording was at the Riverside Studios on 21st November 1963 and it was done with Liverpool accents. Well, it was the time of the Beatles.

Dick was very pleased with the final result and so were his bosses. April 1964 was to see the first transmission of BBC2 and material was needed to fill it. Bill Cotton, then in charge of the director's course, rushed into Michael Peacock's office, 16mm film projector in his hand, and said, 'You must see this!', and he showed the film on the wall of the chief of programmes' office. Michael Peacock thought it might go for a series, and sent for Dick and Ian.

'Do you feel the idea is strong enough for a series?' he said.

'Oh yes, we've always seen it as a series,' said Dick. He lied. 'Id like to commission three episodes,' said Michael Peacock, 'with an option for a further three.'

How did they leave that office on the fourth floor of the Television Centre and begin the walk along that circular corridor to the lifts? Suddenly they were professional writers and had to deliver three scripts, possibly six!

And the title? Nowadays I seem to see 'Likely Lad' in lots of newspaper headlines about a footballer or pop hopeful. In 1964, Dick explained it in promotional material before the series was shown. 'In the North, old men in factories . . . shake their heads watching the younger lads, the apprentices. "There's a likely 'un." It can be said with malice or affection, "Likely" can qualify for good or bad.'

Three scripts were submitted and received a favourable response. In a memo to Tom Sloan, head of Light Entertainment dated 8th July 1964, Duncan Wood confirmed the scripts had arrived and a decision was required as the 'authors are willing and anxious to commence work on the next scripts'. In a further memo six days later, Duncan said, 'On the quality of the writing so far, I think there is no question other than we should take up the option forthwith.' Tom Sloan agreed and Dick and Ian went ahead on the final three scripts. A pattern was created . . . Ian pacing and Dick slaving at the foolscap block. Ian said it gave him time to think and, besides, 'Dick's got better handwriting.' Every few pages they would stop and read the dialogue aloud, getting it right. Journalists would ask me about how much Jimmy and I contributed . . . 'Oh sure, sure . . . a lot . . . up all night, sometimes!'

But we never had to change a comma.

The scripts moved away from Liverpool and across the Pennines. Dick got out a map (typical of Dick to have a map) and a line was drawn from Sunderland, where Jimmy Bolam comes from, to Bingley in Yorkshire, where I come from, and sort of halfway was Middlesbrough, so no one had to put on an accent – important as the word 'real' kept creeping in. Nowadays we are used to regional accents, from sports commentators and newsreaders, even on *The Archers*, whereas in 1964, it, gave the show a freshness.

There was very little money in the kitty for trips up north to film exteriors, but we didn't need to go very far from the Television Centre in west London. We found the ideal location at a place called Willesden Junction. Rows of back-to-back houses like the credits of *Coronation Street* with alleys running behind mean yards with little sentry-box brick outside loos – just like where my grandad lived. At the end of the alleys stood a fence of upright railway sleepers, propping up an embankment to a canal . . . perfect!

There were so many things I loved about those first six scripts. I loved the fact that you saw their workplace at Ellison's factory and saw them at work on their bench. Saw their homes and their mums . . . Terry's mum was to be Olive Milbourne, and she was perfect . . . same shape as my mum, fussing around Terry asking him if he'd wiped his shoes. Another bonus was Sheila Fearn, cast as Terry's sister. Though she didn't always have a lot of dialogue, she made her mark. I enjoyed doing scenes with Sheila (she could throw away a line with the best of them). Then there were the guys we worked with at Ellison's factory. There was Donald McKillop, who was our foreman, always wry and funny (I had worked with him on a radio play two years earlier), and Bartlett Mullins as the father of the maintenance shop where we worked. He was a pet, eyes always twinkling.

Veteran producer Harry Carlisle was assigned to the show, but was unable to do it. Duncan Wood, who had done *Hancock's Half Hour,* couldn't or wouldn't do it, but he suggested that Dick could do it. Duncan thought Dick had done such a great job on the training film.

So to Dick's utter amazement he was offered the chance. A huge bonus for Dick was Sydney Lotterby, already an experienced producer in his own right, but happy to act as Dick's production assistant to help the new boy.

The first episode was recorded on 31st October 1964. I think

Jimmy and I were both wary of the studio audience. *Steptoe and Son* had a studio audience, as did *Hancock's Half Hour*. Tony Hancock used to play to them, and was allowed asides coming out of the plot. But we were proper actors.

I've since seen many a good actor being 'real' in the rehearsal room, then play to the studio audience and forget the camera.

I asked my agent, Peter Crouch, to that very first recording and he brought the actor and director Bill Fraser. Bill was a veteran in sitcoms, *The Army Game* and *Bootsie and Snudge* for Granada Television, and I valued his opinion. We met up afterwards in The Club, the Television Centre bar on the fourth floor.

'Well, what did you think?'

Bill Fraser grinned and in an avuncular, knowing way, said: 'The monster has begun!'

The Likely Lads, BBC2's first situation comedy, went out at 9.55pm on 16th December 1964. BBC2's coverage of the country was gradual. Even if you lived in an area where they received the signal, that didn't guarantee you could get the channel, because a new-style aerial was required.

But the bosses at the BBC were pleased and Michael Peacock was convinced it would be a ratings winner. He said: '*The Likely Lads* stood out from other situation comedies, they were refreshingly sharp and contemporary, and it was terrific to find something you reckon will be a hit.'

Our first episode was well received, and Frank Muir, assistant head at BBC Light Entertainment said: 'It had a remarkable reception. Its ratings on the audience reaction index soared up and up; the last episode reached the highest figure we have ever had.'

Maurice Wiggin wrote in the *Sunday Times,* 'Ian La Frenais and Dick Clement have created a pair who are not only credible, but precisely complementary . . . the happy fact that they are rooted in life, true to life and to themselves.'

Now we had a big break. *The Likely Lads* was to be on BBC1 on Christmas Day in 1964. It was a five-minute sketch.

RADIO TIMES, 25th December 1964

7.15

CHRISTMAS NIGHT WITH THE STARS

A Specially Recorded Programme Featuring Your

Favourite Light Entertainment Artists

INTRODUCED BY JACK WARNER

THE BLACK AND WHITE MINSTRELS	**TERRY SCOTT AND HUGH LLOYD**
ROY CASTLE	**KATHY KIRBY**
BILLY COTTON and his Band	**THE LIKELY LADS**
DICK EMERY	**ANDY STEWART**
BENNY HILL	**TOP OF THE POPS** Greet the Groups

The programme was seen by nineteen million viewers and introduced us to a much wider audience. Ian said: 'That little sketch really started everything off.' It was as if people suddenly said, 'What's this?'

The sketch was about *Rupert* annuals. Well, it was really about a competition, to see who could remember the most about the *Rupert* stories, to kill a bit of time before the pubs opened on Christmas Eve.

Of course *Rupert* was a strip cartoon in the *Daily Express* and every Christmas an annual came out. The old annuals used in the sketch belonged to Nina,who had written in the front 'This book belongs to Nina Bewes'.

AUDREY: Ee you two are smart tonight.

TERRY: Christmas do in the Fat Ox!

BOB: Nice to make an effort.

AUDREY: *You* look very nice, Bob.

BOB: So do you, Audrey.

AUDREY: (TO TERRY) Just come in quietly and don't knock over the hallstand!

(SHE GOES)

BOB: (BY THE TREE) I always had a stocking!

TERRY: Aye, me 'n' all. Me Dad used to creep in. I could smell his breath, leave me stocking and then fall down the stairs and knock over the hallstand . . . blind drunk.

BOB: Happy days.

TERRY: I always had a stocking and a *Rupert* annual.

BOB: Aye, I remember Rupert! The little bear.

TERRY: You should do, you look like him!

BOB: Gerrrraway.

TERRY: Happy days . . . I remember he had a friend, er, Edward, Edward the Elephant.

BOB: It was Edward Trunk!

TERRY: Edward the ELEPHANT!

BOB: It was Edward Trunk!

TERRY: Look man, I had a *Rupert* annual till I was six. It was Edward the Elephant!

BOB: I had one till I was sixteen! Edward Trunk.

TERRY: IT WAS Edward the rotten Elephant!!

BOB: Ten bob on it?

TERRY: Right, you're on! Ten bob . . .

(SEGUE THROUGH ON CHRISTMAS TREE, TIME PASSING, THE BOYS HAVE THEIR JACKETS OFF, TIES UNDONE, TERRY HAS *RUPERT* ANNUAL OPEN IN FRONT OF HIM.)

TERRY: Right, RIGHT! You'll never guess this one. Who, who was in 'Rupert And The Flying Carpet'?

BOB: (QUICKLY ANSWERS) Agly the Pug, Pong Ping The Pekinese, Tiger Lily, and . . . AND Edward Trunk!

TERRY: Oh well, what's the point! What's the point in playing with an ex-Queen's Scout.

BOB: That's five pounds you owe me!

TERRY: You'll get your money; you'll get your money!

(BOB OPENS AN ANNUAL)

BOB: (SMUG) Right . . . who was in 'Rupert's Magic Garden'?

TERRY: Well, there was er . . . Rupert . . .

(BOB REACTS)

TERRY: (CONT.) There was Rupert . . . and er Rupert's dad, and er, that Chinese bit, er . . .

(AUDREY PUTS HER HEAD AROUND THE DOOR)

AUDREY: Does Algy the Pug and *Edward* Trunk know the
            pubs closed ten minutes ago?
(REACTION FROM THE LADS – MUSIC)

THE END

As with most successful shows, publicity and interest from the media and the public escalated as the series evolved. Although it had been well received on its original screening on BBC2, it wasn't until the series was repeated three months later on BBC1 in the prime slot of 8pm that it really took off. By the end of the run it was watched in ten million homes. If there were two people at home, I worked out (with pencil and paper . . .), that was twenty million viewers, nearly half the population of the country!

The *Daily Sketch* said: 'This is the first show since *Steptoe* to say consistently true and funny things about life.'

Barry Took said that: 'Ian La Frenais and Dick Clement became one of the best writing teams ever in television. When *The Likely Lads* was written, there was great competition in script writing, with people like Galton and Simpson, Esmonde and Larby, Feldman and myself – everyone was writing good stuff. Dick and Ian came into the melting pot and held their own. Bewes and Bolam were perfect and the whole concept was right.'

These various pairs of writers always amused me as I got to know them a little better. There always seemed to be the 'straight man' and the 'swinger', just like Dick and Ian. Barry Took, the grown-up, and Marty Feldman, the raver. Dick, the Citroen Safari Estate, and Ian, the red Sunbeam Alpine!

To celebrate the first series, Ian took everybody to Parks, a posh restaurant in London's Beauchamp Place. I remember thinking that it was the kind of place about which my grandad would say: 'Cost you ten bob to spit before you've taken your cap off.'

The first episode of that first series, called *Entente Cordiale,* has the lads returning from their first holiday abroad to Spain, in a railway station buffet, at King's Cross, complete with souvenir sombreros.

BOB: It was pointless you going abroad. You made no attempt, no attempt to speak the language, eat the food and drink the wine. Who was it? Who . . . you met on the beach? Rita from Barrow-in-Furness!

TERRY: She was all right, Rita!

BOB: (CONTEMPT) Yes, but just look at them, English girls abroad, with their peeling shoulders and flowery dresses, like wallpaper on the march.

TERRY: She'd never have done in Barrow-in-Furness what she did in Tossa del Mar.

Episode Two, called *Double Date*, Dick thought the weakest. In Episode Three *Older Women Are More Experienced*, Terry is asked round to the new canteen manageress's house to do a 'little job'. He finds himself under the kitchen sink fixing the pipes. Bob arrives, bringing home his date, the manageress's daughter, who happens to be fourteen!

In number four, *The Other Side of the Fence*, Bob is kicked upstairs for a trial in a white-collar job. He asks Terry to the office social, a mistake. Bob reveals, for the first time, his desire to better himself. Terry's prejudices come out and he's asked to leave. Bob leaves with him, telling his new boss where to stick his job. They head for the

Black Lion and the two secretaries they've been chatting up come too.

Episode Five, *Chance of a Lifetime* has the lads meet a man and his daughter from Adelaide in the Station Hotel. The man extols the virtues of life Down Under. It's only ten pounds state-assisted passage. All the lads have to do is raise the money. He turns out to be a fraud.

Episode Six, *The Suitor*: where Terry Collier's prejudices really come to the fore. His sister is dating Mario, a hairdresser! . . . enough said. Mario turns out to be Ernie from Hull. He plays rugby and darts and likes a pint, and so everything turns out all right in the end. Terry says: 'Hairdressers, Italians, people from Hull – they're all the same.'

The first series came to an end on 20th January 1965. We had had a great press – terrific write-ups. Dick and Ian's careers had kick-started in top gear. There was talk about the series being repeated in March on BBC1.

Nina and I bought a house in Mill Hill, North London, a detached Edwardian house not far from the shops on Mill Hill Broadway, and nearby was the Mill Hill Services Club, an 'All Affiliated' working-men's club. There were four snooker tables and a long bar!

I had always lived in basements or attics; now I had a staircase. The first week I was putting out the rubbish when the dustbin men came,

'Ello . . . know who you are . . . whatsisname, innit?'

'Oh, or huh . . . yeah'

'Yeah, the likelies. Never miss it mate!'

'Oh, er, we've just moved in. I must say it's very nice here . . . I'm thinking of joining the club, the workingmen's club, down the road.'

'You'll never get in!'

'You what?'

'No, You have to be seconded and proposed by a member. They'll never let you in.'

'Oh...'

They were off down the road shouting and banging the bins about. I asked the milkman about it when he came.

'S'full up, I think. There's a waiting list.'

I asked the butcher in Mill Hill Broadway.

'I'll see what I can do, I have some influence in that direction. What does your father do?'

I was eventually proposed by the butcher and seconded by Len Mills, the milkman. Mind you, I had to go for an interview in a sort of board-room off the main room of the club. I stood in a suit and tie, hands behind my back in front of a large oval table. Around the table sat a group of local dignitaries, with pints of beer in front of them. In a tall-backed chair in the centre was our butcher, next to him the milkman.

'Now, we've never had any rough stuff here, no fighting!'

Did I look like a fighter?

'George Zelleski [the foreman of the dustmen] has spoken up for you, and Len here [the milkman], and as I say, we don't entertain trouble here, all right?'

I wondered if they thought I was a 'hell-raiser'? Perhaps they had read about Richard Harris, Nicol Williamson and Oliver Reed?

I said, 'I'm a man of peace, me. I abhor violence.'

I was in and welcomed to the long bar, subsidised beer and spirits . . . my first club!

Friday, 5th March 1965 at 8pm, the first series of *The Likely Lads* was on BBC1. Bob and Terry were becoming household names.

I was mobbed by a screaming horde of schoolgirls! Yes! A screaming horde of schoolgirls in uniform. After appearing on the BBC stand at the Ideal Home Exhibition, I managed to get myself trapped down a corridor with schoolgirls waiting at each end. When they saw me and screamed, I panicked, and they were upon me. I was down, they were screaming, I was screaming . . . Suddenly uniformed security men were dragging me free and hustling me to safety. Smelling-salts and a nurse were sent for.

'Sorry about that, lad, you all right?' said one of the security men. 'Shouldn't wander off, you know. Could have been very nasty . . .'

I was livid. 'Oh, why did you stop it?' I said. 'Can I go back?'

Series Two was recorded through April and May, and began broadcasting on BBC2 on 16th June. Episode Seven was called, *Baby it's Cold Outside*: Terry and Bob have a date with two nurses. Where to take them? The lads agree to babysit for Jack (Donald McKillop, their foreman at work). They tell the girls it's their flat, but then the baby starts crying. The girls naturally spend the whole evening cooing over the kiddie (Clement Junior).

In Episode Eight, *A Star is Born*, about a pub talent competition, I wear sunglasses and sing Roy Orbison's 'Pretty Woman'. Everyone said I looked like Roy Orbison, but I think they were just being rude.

Episode Nine was called *The Talk of the Town*: the morning after the night before, Bob goes to work and can't understand why everyone is congratulating him. Then they remind him of last night's party where he stood on the sideboard and proposed to Helen, and put a ring on her finger! Helen was Helen Fraser who had been in *Billy Liar*.

In Episode Ten, the beautiful Wanda Ventham (fancy going out with a Wanda . . . ?) and Wendy Richard were sales demonstrators in a store (I think this was a fantasy of Ian's, you know, like those beautifully made-up girls who sell perfume in Harrods). The lads are determined to get a date and so buy most of their stock. Episode Eleven, *Faraway Places* is all about moonlighting, searching for an extra job to afford a holiday. They've spent too much on Wanda and Wendy the week before. At the Labour Exchange, all Terry's bitterness comes out, Property is Theft, the Jarrow Marchers, etc, etc. In the twelfth episode, *Where Have All the Flowers Gone?*, the lads go to a wedding – a mistake! Everyone, aunts, friends and parents can't stop themselves saying . . . 'I expect it'll be one of you two next?' Even Aunty Peggy says it's about time they settled down. The lads are fed up with everyone wondering when they'll get hitched. 'I expect it'll be one of you two next!' Terry is holding an inverted half grapefruit full of sticks holding little sausages.

TERRY: The next person who says that . . .! Is going to get
            this right up his . . .
VICAR: Hello boys, I expect it'll be one of you two next?
TERRY: . . . sausage, Vicar?

The last line delivered with an angry look only Bolam can do.

Chapter 14

WHILE I WAS busy being a household name Nina ran away to Cornwall.

My friend Roy Battersby, my best man and by now a director at Thames Television, was away in America. He'd told me to be sure to ring his wife Audrey and ask her out. So we went to the Ad Lib club, high above Leicester Square. The Ad Lib was the very first discothèque and I still think the best. It was five or six storeys above the Prince Charles Cinema, between Leicester Square and Lisle Street.

The night I took Audrey, the place was humming, The sunken dance floor was packed. On the terrace surrounding the dance floor the tables were all full and behind them, the windows looked out on the panoramic view of the London skyline. That night you could see as far as Parliament Hill Fields.

The waiter came and took our order. A half bottle of Mateus Rosé, please.

Well, this was 1965.

A waiter poured the wine and 'Baby love, oh Baby Love' played in the background.

'Wanna dance?'

'No thank you, Rodney'

Had someone told her? Then the waiter was back at my side. 'Excuse me, Mr McCartney wants to know if you'll have a drink on him?'

'Oh, sure, certainly like . . . another half of Mateus Rosé, ta.'

Audrey was amazed. 'Is it really . . . where? You sure he means us?'

'Yeah, sorry about that Aud, s'always happening.' (He shrugs his shoulders, looking for a cool he never had.)

'Oh wait till Roy hears about this!'

'Sure you don't wanna dance?'

'Positive luv . . . Ian told me.'

'Oh . . .'

The waiter was back with the second half of Mateus Rosé, courtesy of Paul McCartney. 'Mr McCartney asks would you like to join him and Miss Asher?'

'Oh, sure, sure. Tell him, yeah.'

As we approached their table on the raised level at the back, me clutching two half bottles of Mateus Rosé like a pair of maracas, Paul and Jane stood up. 'Er, I love the series, man! S'great really!'

'Oh, I, er . . . this is Audrey, she's not me . . . er . . . she's . . .'

'Sit down, sit down. This is Jane.'

'Hello, how are you?'

'Thanks for the er . . . I saw you at ATV. Eric Morecambe took me into your studio, his studio. *The Morecambe and Wise Show.* You were on it.'

'Oh yeah?'

'Yeah, last year, the beginning of '64.'

'It was a good year for us.'

'It was a good year for us too, Paul.'

★

Off screen something had begun to happen that has stayed with me until this day. People often called out to me in the street, 'Where's Terry, then?' or 'Where's your mate?'

Jimmy Bolam used to tell them I was dead. When I remonstrated, he said, 'Saves all argument mate, stops 'em in their tracks. "He's dead" I say, and they just stand there with their mouths open. Don't ask for your autograph, nothing, end of conversation.'

I've known quite a few actors who 'Don't do interviews'. Strange how they change when they have a percentage of the box office of a stage play, so ticket sales are reflected in their pay packets. Then it's: 'What can we do to publicise the play?'

Throughout 1965 I seemed to be forever on television and always being interviewed. I had to do most of the publicity for *The Likely Lads* as Jimmy Bolam was averse to it, which is putting it mildly. He once told journalist Lynda Lee-Potter:

'Look, I'm having some new track rods fitted on my car. I don't want to know anything about the man who's doing it. Why should he want to know about me?'

In all my interviews Nina was mentioned less and less. She was still in Cornwall and I stayed in Chelsea with Tom Courtenay or with Ian La Frenais.

In September I arrived in Dublin. I was going to be at the Gaiety Theatre doing *Little Malcolm and his Struggle against the Eunuchs*.

I had really enjoyed Dublin in 1961 in the Pinter play. Now on the quay in the pouring rain, I found a jolly taxi driver, but his cab slowly came to a halt in the middle of the road, halfway to Dublin.

'ARRGH! Jesus Mary and Joseph, haven't I run out of petrol?'

When we did eventually get to Dublin, I went to see the theatre and then found my way into Neary's Bar beside the Gaiety. An ancient man in an old ex-army greatcoat asked me, 'Ah God bless you captain, will yus buy us a drink?' And when I obliged, 'May all the saints plant a flower on yer head . . . let yer footsteps be dogged by the stars o'luck!'

Most nights, straight after the final curtain, I would go out the stage door and there God bless me, almost directly opposite, was the back door of Neary's. I would pull open the door and look along that beautiful long bar with its chrome Corinthian columns surmounted by rows of globes lighting up the crowded pub, people fighting to get a drink. Over the whole scene I would shout, 'Michael, get us a PINT.'

And Michael would stop what he was doing and start pouring a long, creamy pint of cool Guinness. Then . . .

'Pass that to d'lad at d'door! He's from d'theatre, make way, make way, there! Pay us after, mate!'

I'd take my pint up to my dressing-room, take off my make-up, change my clothes and think, what if I did that in London, in say, St Martin's Lane at The Salisbury at theatre closing time? I'd be thrown out on my ear into the street! Or just ignored.

I love Dublin.

We used to meet at Tom's house, a little gang of us, to go to football. Ian (Newcastle United), Tom (Hull City, 'Come on the Tigers!'), and me (Chelsea, 'Come on you Blues!'). But one Saturday Tom didn't want to go.

The film of *Billy Liar* was on at cinemas all over. 'No, you see it's different now,' he said. 'I just don't feel I can go, you know, and stand at the Shed End as we have done, er . . . now.'

We told him not to be so daft and made him come, reluctantly . . . off t'match.

We used to stand, oh, about halfway up the terracing up behind the goal but a bit to the side. This Saturday, the crowd was filling up the ground when a lad, way down to our left near the touch line, stared up at us, and shouted, 'Billy Liar!'

Tom, ashen, grim. 'Oh hell, I told you, I said . . . didn't I? Shouldn't have . . . er!'

Again, loudly, 'Billy Liar!'

'Oh Christ! I knew it would be like . . . bloody hell.'

I said, calmly, 'Tom? Tom, all you have to do is smile. Give him a little smile perhaps a little wave . . . all over, OK?'

'Eh, Billy Liar!'

Tom dutifully tried a very little smile, more a grimace than a smile. The bloke threw half an orange that hit Tom smack in the face.

So perhaps his first instinct had been right.

Chapter 15

THE LOVELY LESLEY from Linlithcow was a graphic artist at Granada Television. She made me a first-night present for the London run of *Little Malcolm*. It read 'Good Luck' in sequins that caught the lights and trembled. George Harrison came on the first night with Patti Boyd. In fact the first week everybody came, Paul and Jane, Ringo, John, Brian Epstein, Peter O'Toole, Peter Blake, Sir Alec Guinness and Sir Laurence Olivier.

I took the Sunday papers. Penelope Gilliat in the *Observer* said: 'Rodney Bewes in a beautifully low-key comic performance.' *Little Malcolm and his Struggle Against the Eunuchs* came off after two weeks. Michael Codron said: 'No public response, my dears. Only took £60 some nights, but it was a *succès d'estime.*'

I was sad about Nina. We met for lunch at San Lorenzo, Knightsbridge. She said she wanted us to try again, to get back together. I knew it was impossible, because I was with Lesley now. We were both near to tears. Lorenzo came and sat with us, bringing a bottle of fine Armagnac brandy.

I have a letter from Nina, written many years later, trying to make things clear . . . very real, very touching.

I was so young, so immature, no experience, unworldly. I had been nowhere, seen nothing of men. Just school (all girls), holidays in Cornwall where I met someone who wanted me when I was fifteen. Then university, then I fell in love with this man with big brown eyes and a soft velvet voice. I was the happiest girl in the world. You were my first boyfriend, the first man . . . I loved you very much and, I might add, never stopped loving you. So why? We hardly saw each other.

This was true, I thought, after we had been married such a very short time, I had gone off to tour South America and Europe for five months.

I had to go to bed early, to go to school and teach. You were always out. The more famous you became the less I saw of you, and when we were together there was a new presence in our marriage – Joe Public. Everywhere we went 'they' were there and 'they' wanted you and loved you too. I felt alone. I just cut and RAN. The only man I knew in the world didn't notice me anymore, need me anymore. I ran to the only person who had noticed me before. Oh, what a mistake!

Tom was taking me to supper in a Chelsea restaurant with Sir Alec Guinness. Tom warned me in the car not to let him down in front of Sir Alec. 'Watch your language . . . Oh, and there's no need to overdo it . . . to come over . . . northern like . . .'

Sir Alec was fond of Tom, I could see. He didn't say if he'd seen *The Likely Lads*. After a while I found myself calling him S'Alec, all one word, sort of Alec with a sibilant S. We were talking about keeping fit. I said, 'Oh, S'Alec, we've started playing football in Hyde Park, Sunday mornings.'

Disapproving look from Tom. He's such a 'head boy' . . .

'Oh, really? I am just around the corner, Prince's Gate, Ennismore Gardens, I must come and have a knock-about . . . kick-about, ha, ha!'

I don't think he meant it. But Rod Steiger said he would come, if we showed him the rules. He lived near the Park too, with Claire Bloom, his wife.

Staying at Tom's, I went to collect the post. He was still in bed. 'Eeh, there's a package from . . . from the Academy of Motion Picture Arts and Sciences . . . from LA! . . . Los Angeles, California, USA.'

Tom seemed uninterested. 'Uh huh. You don't say,' he said with what may have been an attempt at an American drawl.

'Oh, I say! Shall we open it?' I said – irrepressibly.

'You open it . . . I'm not bothered . . . you can . . . if you, er . . .'

Tom has this habit of leaving sentences unfinished, up in the air . . . Assuming you know what is coming next:

'Did you get the . . . for Saturday?'

'Yeah, the tickets? Chelsea–Hull City, certainly.'

'Ah, . . .did you . . .?'

'Yes, I got four.'

I opened the package. It was an oblong plaque, shiny varnish, gilt lettering on gloss black background. And there was that famous logo . . .

'Oh, oh it says it's from the Oscars! It says you've been nominated for an Oscar for *Doctor Zhivago*.'

'Oh, I knew about that.'

'But what shall I do with it? Don't you want to look at it?'

'Shove it in a drawer, me sock drawer, you know.'

On Saturday, we had planned a Dads day out, both Dads coming to London. I met my father at Mill Hill and we were to meet Tom Courtenay senior (both Courtenays are called Tom) at King's Cross at one o'clock, then off t'match. We took our seats quite low down on the west stand. As we came down all those long steps, slowly, for Tom's dad had a gammy leg, I noticed a familiar face, and smiled back. We found our seats, and I leaned across the two dads and grabbed Tom's arm.

'Hey, hey, hey, do you know who's a few rows back, up behind us? Sir Len Hutton.'

'No . . . never,' said Tom's dad.

Tom turned around in his seat and gave Len Hutton a cheery wave. Tom got a smile and a wave back and told the dads, who were both visibly expanding with pride.

Just before half-time Chelsea were two up so I had a big grin on my face.

Tom scowled. 'Don't smile!'

He gave the second word five syllables.

But the final score was two each, so all was forgiven before our evening out at the Mill Hill Services Club, where Tom senior was very much at home. So was my dad, playing darts with Len Mills, the milkman and big George Zelleski, the dustman.

Big George just about to throw his first arrow: 'You, you er . . . working at the moment, Tom?'

'Oh, er no. Not at the er . . . moment.'

There's me thinking, no, but he's just been nominated for an Oscar for *Doctor Zhivago,* mate!

Big George threw his second dart. 'Well, that's the trouble with your game, innit?'

He threw his third dart. 'It's not regular!'

At the Television Centre, in the foyer, waiting to go off to film the third series of *The Likely Lads,* the newly appointed Controller of BBC2, David Attenborough came towards Jimmy and me, beaming: 'Hello, hello, I'm so proud, proud I've inherited you two!' Jimmy said, 'Who are you?'

We were to do eight episodes of *The Likely Lads,* and Episode Fourteen *Friends and Neighbours* had a very special guest star! Wilfred Lawson was to be Terry's grandfather. Wilfred was so right for the part. He'd done it all, Hollywood, British films, the theatre, I had seen him in *The Prisoner* with Sir Alec Guinness, being wonderful as the jailer.

But what about his reputation for being cantankerous?

Going to do pre-filming with Wilfred was an adventure. We had a car and Geoffrey, our regular driver. Looking for the suburban location, we stopped at a country club.

'Come on, Wilfred, we are going to have a swift half, me and Jimmy and the driver.'

How do you describe what Wilfred was like? Crotchety? Maybe, but he was certainly rather frail. This was to be his last job, although we didn't know that.

'No, I don't want to come with you and the driver . . . you go and leave me . . . I'm going in the public bar and you go in the other . . . there, all right?'

Was he objecting to the driver coming too? Surely not? Jimmy knew instinctively how to speak to him. It was remarkable. 'Don't be such a silly old sod, you do as you're told. Get in there . . . now!'

And, meekly, he came with us and seemed pleased that someone was being firm with him.

At the studio Wilfred was an old hand with the audience. He began to turn around a lot of his lines to get a laugh, or failing that, to make *us* laugh. With a wicked glint in his eye, a line I had heard for a week in the rehearsal room, as 'If that woman comes around my front door again, she'll get my fist in her face!' became on the recording: 'If that woman comes around my front door any more she'll get my thingammybob in her gob, Bob!'

Then he gave Jimmy and me that wicked look, hoping we'd fall about laughing. When we were solid, that made him even worse.

'Stay to tea, Bob, we've got some Hungarian gherkins' became 'Stay fer tea, Bobby . . . you can have a nibble of me gherkin!'

And he had started winking, now . . .!

Episode Fifteen, *Rocker*, was a lot of fun. Bob has wheels! He's bought a second-hand scooter. Terry helps Bob, quizzing him on the Highway Code . . . I remember in 1966 the Highway Code still had pictures of a man on a cart driving his horse, and illustrations of said carter, his arm up holding his whip which described an anti-clockwise circle to indicate he was turning left!

The best bit, visually, in *Rocker* was Terry helping Bob practise an emergency stop for his test. Terry is delegated to leap out from behind a parked car, arm outstretched and shout 'STOP!' As Bob drives away around the block, a scooter appears, Terry jumps out arm raised, and the speeding scooter runs slap into him . . . then around the corner wobbles our Bob to view the scene in horror . . . And the cut is to HOSPITAL WARD INTERIOR, DAY: Attractive nurse comes towards Terry in a starched uniform with little silver upside-down watch on her left breast.

She was played by Carol Mowlam, not that I remember, oh yes I do, to this day.

Then we were off, filming on location to do *Anchors Aweigh* on the Norfolk Broads. Syd Lotterby handed out train tickets, we had to be at Liverpool Street Station at 9.30 on Tuesday morning.

'Why can't we go first class, Dick?'

'Oh, I don't know, it's the BBC, you know.'

'We ought to have a compartment to ourselves, first class. I mean we're famous now.'

Syd said, 'No one gets first class travel, ever, I mean Richard Dimbleby . . . even.'

'Oh, I feel like . . . they make me feel like . . . a used sock.'

I saw a huge hoarding at Norwich Station: WELCOME TO NORWICH, GATEWAY TO THE BROADS. I wondered what Americans made of it.

We were put up at The Swan at Horning. The crew, everybody had a party that first lunchtime. We weren't filming until the next day, so we had what the lads in the village in Cornwall call a 'Sod It'. When the weather is too rough to go fishing, they say 'Sod it' and go to the pub instead. The landlord of The Swan asked me what I was drinking.

'Have you a presumptuous claret, mine host?'

'I've got a very nice red in the cellar. I'm going to bring up a bottle just for you. I'll put it here on the bar behind this pillar, I'll shove the cork in and you just help yourself through the week.'

It was a very nice claret, so much so that that lunchtime we went through eleven bottles of it. I think Dick and the cameraman, Elmer Cossey, had to go and look at the location that afternoon, but the rest of us stayed in The Swan.

'You coming, Ian?' asked Dick. 'To look at the boat, the location?'

'Oh no, s'alright, Dick, you go. I'll stay with the lads.'

We played bar billiards, skittles and darts. The place seemed full of holidaymakers from the north. One in braces and flat cap, said, 'Ee by heck, seeing you two . . . I thought I'd brought me telly with me!'

In *Anchors Aweigh* our boat is stuck fast on a mud flat all night. Terry furious, Bob happily whittling a stick with his ex-Queen's Scout penknife.

BOB: Eh, look, those geese are back!

TERRY: Oh wonderful, the geese are back!

BOB: No, they're very interesting, those geese . . . they'll be off soon, off to North America.

TERRY: Lucky bloody geese!

I saw a possibility at the end of one scene and asked Dick quietly, away from Jimmy, not to say 'cut' at the end, to keep it running. The shot began tight on a bucket and a mop, widening to show Bob swabbing the decks. Down from the bows I mopped the deck between the cabin side and the edge of the boat till I got to the cockpit, pushing my bucket along with my foot mopping away cheerfully until I picked up the bucket and tipped it over the side. Terry emerges from the cabin, cross at still being aground, with a cigarette in his mouth. He scowls at his little friend.

On 'Action' along the deck I came, a happy soul, Bob doing his mopping, until I got to the stern of the boat then, just as Terry came through a little door to the cockpit and stood up, I threw my bucket of water across the other side and over his face. He was livid, water dripping down his face and his mouth open, and the fag stayed stuck to his bottom lip . . . a bonus.

Jimmy's look was – oh . . . it couldn't have been more wonderful and it slowly changed as he began to realise I had planned it. It became a slow burn worthy of that one-eyed take James Finlayson does in Laurel and Hardy films. The crew, everyone, just fell apart, and Jimmy took it in very good part. He knew it was so right for the scene. He even agreed to a covering close-up, dripping water again and this time the make-up lady sticking a half-smoked ciggy to his bottom lip with spirit gum . . . you can't get more dedicated than that.

Back to reality on Friday. Well not really, Ian and I were off to Paris to spend the weekend with Tom . . . in Omar Sharif's flat! We drove into Paris that evening, the lights twinkling, a beautiful June evening. Tom said: 'Er, this flat I share with Omar, well, er, look I know I don't have to say this to you, Ian, but, I mean Omar's sophisticated and, er, what I'm saying is . . .'

Ian and Rodney together: 'Don't let us down!'

Honestly, only Tom!

'No, only we're having a 'do' tomorrow night, a party at the flat. I just thought I would mention . . . ?'

'We won't let you down, Tom.'

'No, we'll be on our best behaviour.'

'Clean hanky . . . clean pants, in case, like!'

'In case we get run over by a Paris bus.'

'In case we score!'

We dropped our bags and Tom took us to Castile for supper. I woke up the next morning at 10 Avenue Foch, to a polite tap, tap-tapping on the door.

'May I come in?'

And there was Omar with a lovely smile, arm out to shake hands, then he sat on the end of my bed. 'Did you sleep well? I've come to ask, to say welcome and ask how would you like coffee? An egg? How would you like it?'

All I could think of was, what a charmer, what a gentleman.

'Tom's told me so much about you. It's good to have friends to stay. Now, one egg or two?'

Discovering the flat, I found it wasn't a flat but rather an apartment on more than one floor, and really it wasn't an apartment, it was a museum. The first-floor living-room, I mean, drawing-room, I mean salon, had long windows to the floor with long gilt mirrors between them and the chimney piece was held by two great marble caryatids. I expect there is an identical room at Versailles. And through the tall windows, a park, and up away to the left was l'Arc de Triomphe.

Ian suggested we could have a kick-about in the Tuileries gardens tomorrow as we would be missing our fixture in Hyde Park.

In the corner of the *grand salon* on the polished parquet floor, stood a very *grand* grand piano, black Chinese lacquer covered in scenes of an eastern garden in gilt and red. It was magnificent. I think being asked not to be embarrassing with our gauche northern ways must have rather got up Ian's nose. Ian may be from Whitley Bay but he has as much sophistication as the next man. Not as much as Omar . . . but as much as the next man.

In the evening they began to arrive: Geraldine Chaplin, and others from Tom's film. Champagne flute in his hand, Ian was leaning against that piano, decorated all over in scenes of old China. He turned to Omar and said, 'Ee, Omar, isn't it terrible what vandals will do? Someone's painted all over your piano!'

Tuesday morning, and I'm back at the Addison Road Boys' Club, in our rehearsal room with Isobel Black who's in this week's episode.

In *Brief Encounter* Isobel Black is playing Ursula, over from west-coast Blackpool, to look after a sick aunt. Both the lads are dating this same girl, but don't know it until the last poignant scene on a railway station platform. Early on in the episode:

TERRY: No . . . I can't tonight, but tomorrow?

BOB: No, I can't tomorrow,

TERRY: I can't Friday.

BOB: But that's Friday. Traditional that is, Friday. Lads' night out.

TERRY: Sorry.

BOB: Yeah. I'm sorry about tomorrow night.

On and off screen everyone's got the hots for Isobel Black.

One day, I drove to Chichester to meet Tom in a lunchtime pub. I sat on a high stool at the bar to wait for him. A woman came in and sat next to me. I was pretending to read a paper when I realised it was Celia Johnson. I heard her say in that voice, so clipped and quick and beautifully articulated, that famous voice from *Brief Encounter* and *In Which We Serve* . . .

'I say, could I have a crab salad? I had one last week, it was frightfully good.'

I was bursting to speak to her. 'Oh, excuse me,' I said. 'I'm here to meet Tom. Tom Courtenay. I'm a friend of his. You're rehearsing with him, er . . . in *The Cherry Orchard*?'

She looked at me as if I was the village idiot.

'Only I just *had* to speak to you, you see I'm an actor.'

She allowed herself a smile. Was she humouring me?

'Yes, and I do a series on television. I'm in a series, er . . . a situation comedy series, on television . . . it's called *The Likely Lads*.'

She said again in that voice from all those patriotic British films with Noël (no one can speak that fast nowadays), 'Oh really? I haven't seen it, is it good?'

'Oh er . . . no, only I had to speak to you, you see. I mean I wouldn't normally, but tomorrow's episode, on television tomorrow, er . . . on BBC2 is called *Brief Encounter*!'

'Oh yes, I do see . . . how amusing.'

'Yes, and it's just that the two, er . . . lads, me and er . . . are going out, seeing the same girl, though they don't know it. That is, until the last scene when they meet to say goodbye to her, on a railway station platform . . . like?'

'Yes.'

I was in trouble, struggling, when into the pub strode John Laurie, who was also in the play with Tom and Celia Johnson. He marched up to us and said, 'Hello Celia.'

Then he turned to me, beaming, and said in the distinctive Scottish accent that would become even more famous when he was in *Dad's Army* for all those years: 'Hello, young man, what a pleasure to meet you. You're a very clever young actor, aren't you!'

I could have kissed him. Now he turned to Celia again: 'He's a very good actor. You have seen *The Likely Lads,* of course? The best thing on the television!'

I was to become great friends with Celia and spend many happy times at her house in Oxfordshire.

On Sunday, I was back to start work on Episode Nineteen, the last we were to record. This week it is *Love and Marriage*. Bob is disillusioned with the job, with the town, with life, in a rut, and he's going to get away from it all. Goodbye . . . take the king's shilling, join up, see the world. He's going to join the army! Terry doesn't believe he'll do it, but he does, and that makes Terry begin to think, and also he misses his little friend. If you can't beat 'em . . . Terry signs on for three years, only to pass, on his way in, Bob on his way out.

EXTERIOR DAY. BOB STANDS AT THE BACK OF ARMY LORRY, TERRY ON PAVEMENT WITH OTHER NEW RECRUITS

TERRY: Where're you off to?
BOB: (SHOUTS) Home!
TERRY: Leave?
BOB: No, I'm out. Discharged!
TERRY: You WHAT? I've just signed on . . . for three years!
BOB: Medical discharge.
TERRY: THREE YEARS!
BOB: Flat feet!
TERRY: Three bloody years . . .

BUT HIS WORDS ARE DROWNED OUT BY THE NOISE OF ARMY LORRY REVVING UP AND DRIVING OFF TAKING BOB TO FREEDOM. CLOSE ON TERRY'S ANGRY FACE CUT BOB LOOKING SURPRISINGLY HAPPY. ROLL FINAL CREDITS.

THE END

Between 1964 and 1966 we had done twenty episodes and one five-minute sketch on *Christmas Night with the Stars*. Now it was all over. The last episode was seen in 13.7 million homes.

Our final party was at Grumbles in Victoria. It was a regular haunt, a place where you might bump into Lennon and McCartney or Albert Finney, or Michael Caine. The mini-skirted waitresses are deadly and unobtainable. That night someone was violently ill and Ian tried to pull Isobel Black. The next morning I drove to Chichester, and that evening Tom and I had dinner at the Old Cross Inn, then went to a disco in an old barn.

The following day, a Sunday, we had tea with John Laurie. Was he ever a young man? Over tea with scones and cream, he interrogated us with his rolling r's Scottish accent.

'And did you two Likely Lads go out rrraving last night? On the town, on the pooooll? Dancin' an' rrrock an' rrrollinn'?'

'We had a quiet dinner at the Old Cross, John. I don't know what you mean . . . raving? No!' said the head boy.

'Then,' I said, 'we went to Tikies Bar and Disco in the Old Barn!'

'Aaaah! And werr therr many mini-skirted young girls therr?' His eyes gleamed with wicked thoughts.

'Hmm yeah, John!'

'Eh, one day man will walk down the King's Road in Chelsea with his flies undone, but proudly!'

★

Everyone was World Cup crazy, including me. I had a World Cup Willy wall chart! I filled in every match, colouring in little footballers with crayons, until it was full up.

I have been asked a few times by journalists, 'Where were you the day we beat West Germany in the World Cup?' and I've always answered 'I can't remember.'

I can, though. I was in Lesley's flat in West Hampstead, in bed with Lesley, watching it on television. 'They think it's all over! Well it is now!!'

England has scored again.

Chapter 16

I WAS FILMING A TV series a bit like *The Saint* and *Danger Man*, made by the same company. It was called *McGill, The Man in a Suitcase*. In Episode Four, *The Bridge*, I'm a suicidal concert pianist!

We filmed on Albert Bridge in Chelsea which is very beautiful, cast-iron.

EXTERIOR, BRIDGE, DAY: We filmed from seven in the morning until late afternoon. I'm supposed to leap off the top of one of the towers that hold the great suspension chains, to my watery grave in the murky waters below.

The first morning, early, the director said to me: 'Rodney, try to keep as low a profile as you can on top of that tower, OK? I don't want cars stopping, rushing off to phone the police, concerned about this guy on top of the bridge.'

But one of the first cars across the bridge was a Morris Minor, with the hood down. Mum and Dad were in the front, two children in the back with the dog. The car stopped. They are all looked up. Dad shouted: 'Eh! You up there!'

Me? I pointed to my chest, me?

'Yes, you! Go on you silly f****r, JUMP!'

*

Tom asked me to go the Royal Court Theatre to see his friend, Sir Alec Guinness in the Scottish play with Simone Signoret as Lady M. The play had had very mixed reviews.

In the first interval, Tom and I went to the hotel bar in Sloane Square to avoid the crush in the theatre bar and there we bumped into Sir Laurence Olivier. He greeted Tom like a long-lost friend. Then I asked him what he wanted to drink, and one of those ridiculous arguments started.

'What will you have, Sir Laurence?'

'No, no, no it's my shout!'

'No, it's my round.'

'No, no, I insist, my round.'

'No, please, Sir Laurence, it's my round.' Oh, Lord, I'm arguing with Sir Laurence Olivier about who's getting them in!

'No, no, no, my round. I'm working!'

I couldn't believe he said that to me. 'So am I! It's my round!' Oh Lord, the interval will be over soon, I was thinking and I'll never get a drink.

Tom intervened. 'I'll get the drinks. Now, what's it to, er . . .'

After the play, and it wasn't good. Sir Alec was in his dressing-room. He was talking to Tom, so I was off the hook. I found a corner to hide, my bum gratefully in the washbasin, but suddenly Sir Alec was asking me something . . .

'And did you see, Rodney? In the first act I dragged my foot across the fore-stage, the action worthy of Stanley Matthews!'

'Oh, oh I thought . . . yes.'

What's he on about? Everyone was looking at me on the washbasin in the corner.

'Er, I remember, I mean you did this wonderful sweeping movement with your foot, er . . . was it about er . . . the impermanence of Dunsinane, er . . . Burnham Wood on the move . . . ?

Sir Alec is looking at me as if I'm round the twist. 'Wretched woman had her programme open on the front of the stage and her fur tippet too. I kicked 'em off. Ha, ha, right into her lap!'

Everyone was laughing and the focus was off me, thank goodness.

Knock, knock and there was my drinking companion from the Sloane Square Hotel bar. I sank deeper into my washbasin.

'Larry, Larry, come in, come in, now you know . . . ?'

'Alec, Alec . . . you were wonderful, magnificent. Mighty! What about supper, I'm taking you to supper, what d'you say?'

'No, no, Larry, most kind, but I'm previously engaged . . . a small "do" for the crew. At Ennismore Gardens, just the stage management and Tom and Rodney.'

'Oh, I say, I'll come too, couldn't I come, Alec? I could be a gatecrasher, couldn't I? Ha, ha.'

And that's just what Sir Laurence did, he gatecrashed Sir Alec's 'do' and Simone Signoret came too.

I thought Sir Laurence made it harder for people to relax.

I was sitting on the sofa with S'Alec, when suddenly, there's Sir Laurence pushing a box of cigarettes under my nose. 'Do have an Olivier?' he said. 'Ha, ha, ha!'

I had read in the paper Gallagher's had paid him £70,000 to use his name on these filter-tipped cigarettes. Without a thought I said, 'I'd rather have a Guinness!'

Sir Alec's eyes twinkled, but Sir Laurence gave me such a look that I felt the bayonet going in and twisting in my gut.

I fled to the kitchen, the empty kitchen to be alone and to take a few deep breaths . . . and suddenly Simone Signoret was there, advancing towards me. I backed towards the fridge. I had seen her in so many French films, and now she wants reassurance from me. At least I think she did. That accent hadn't helped her Lady M, in fact it had been hard to understand her, and now my back was against the refrigerator, and she was very close to me. I couldn't breathe. 'Tell er . . . me Rodnay, er . . . what did you really sink eh? Was eeat really awful, was eeeat so ver, ver awful as terrible as zay are saying, dear boy?'

'No, no, honestly, you were great, really wonderful, marvellous . . . mighty!'

I could smell her breath. Have I got any asthma pills with me? Take me home, Tom! Is she going to kiss me, there, up against the fridge in Sir Alec Guinness's kitchen? What if Lady Guinness comes in? Should I kiss her? Now we *are* kissing, and I am enjoying it. What if Sir Laurence bloody Olivier comes in?

In the car going back to Tom's, I thought it better not to tell him about 'I'd rather have a Guinness'.

Perhaps not tell him about me and Simone either . . . Oh dear.

Tom and I had arranged to see Sir Alec for an early dinner in a smart Chelsea restaurant the following week, after the play had finished at the Royal Court, and on our way there we ran into Celia Johnson.

'Where are you two boys going?'

We told her and, 'Oh, I see, well I'm coming too! Tee, hee! Alec won't mind, he ADORES me!'

And she did come too and, of course, Alec didn't mind and we had a wonderful time. Celia on great form was so funny and clever and bright and loved being with three men. She flirted outrageously. She was like a young girl sometimes even though she was so wise.

Alec told her about 'I'd rather have a Guinness'. He said, 'I've been telling EVERYONE! There'll be no National Theatre for Rodney!'

★

I took a model to dinner. She was black and exotic and I was out of my depth. Back home she was there on the sofa, and while I opened champagne, all I could think was that on my bed were those dark green sheets from Peter Jones! Damn, I can't leave her and go upstairs to change the sheets on the bed just because they are dark green and I've never slept with a black girl and I want the sheets to be white.

Gentle reader, you do understand, don't you? I was a likely lad, for goodness sake!

I was divorced and got custody of the cat. Tom had moved west to a tall house overlooking Hurlingham Park in Fulham and I found a delightful little house in the street behind. I went up to Newcastle, to do a play, in my new white Porsche convertible, all roundy like a dodgem car.

When I returned I found a 'Dear John' letter from Lesley.

I met him only three weeks ago . . . he lives in America . . . if I don't come back in three weeks' time, I shall come back in the autumn as Mrs . . .

Look after yourself, Love, Lesley.

Chapter 17

IN MY NEW house, all alone. I just sat and cried and cried. I realised how much I loved Lesley, should have married her. I had played around, had had a lot of fun. Now she had gone to America. What a fool I had been. Albert, the cat, came in to see what was the matter with me.

I plucked up courage to talk to a Grumbles waitress, deadly as she leaned over in an orange mini-skirt and matching knickers to serve apple crumble to the table opposite. I found out she worked in the evenings and weekends for extra money, and that really she was a designer, so I rang her office.

'How did you get this number?'

'Someone at the restaurant said you worked for JRM Designs. I looked them up.'

'Was it Avril? I'll kill her.'

'Er, d'you want to come to Chelsea, Saturday? It's Chelsea–Stoke City.'

She said yes! I found out later, she regretted it and wanted to get out of it but she couldn't get my number because I was ex-directory.

Daphne designed cardboard furniture and tin tablemats and

coasters. I still have a tin tray all orange and yellow swirls, that says on the back 'Tarragon' a design by Daphne Black. I'm very proud of it and used to show it to everybody that came to the house. She was in a *Sunday Times* colour supplement, her picture on a page headed 'Top Designers of the Sixties', and her cardboard furniture would be exhibited in the Victoria & Albert Museum.

Tom's dad would come to London for long weekends. We had a little routine his son didn't know about. He would come round to my house round the corner for his first roll-up of the day and a blue Bass, kept especially for him.

I could imagine him leaving Tom's house. 'No, just popping out fer a . . . round the . . . breath of . . . no, I won't be . . .'

That no, is a Hull thing. They say no at the start of an affirmative line, like, 'No, I will 'ave a pint ta!' or 'No, it was a lovely meal.' He doesn't finish his sentences either, like Tom. Knock, knock on my front door.

'Hello Rodney, no, I just thought ah . . .?'

'Come in, come in Mr Courtenay.'

At that moment, David Wall, a dancer friend who was staying in my spare room, came tripping down the stairs, in my royal blue dressing-gown, pointing his toes. He was nicknamed Ginger because of his red hair. I said, 'This is Ginger, Mr Courtenay, remember I told you all about him?'

'Oh aye?' said Tom's dad, giving me a long look.

'I'll just pop into the kitchen,' said Ginger with a great grin. 'Then I'll come back and say hello properly.'

I took Tom's dad into the living-room and out came the tobacco tin as he started the ritual of making a roll-up. 'No, is that that ballet dancer you told me of? No . . . I mean 'ave got nowt . . . er no.'

The first ballet dancer he had ever met. You don't get many dancers off the Hessle Road in Hull.

'Yes, he's a principal dancer with the Royal Ballet, and his wife's upstairs, his *wife*, Freda . . . she's upstairs like.'

On hearing this – 'NO, when I was a lad we used to think tennis players were peculiar!'

That early autumn of 1968 I was ill. It started with a cold, then flu and I was in bed for ten days anyway, so it was a bad 'do' as we say up north. Albert, the cat, came and sat on my bed every day. He's not the kind of cat to come and sit on your lap and purr, but I did discover he was stalwart at times of serious illness in the house.

Being ill in bed, I had time to write. I didn't write home that I was ill, no point really, as my mother would have been down on the next train. This is what I wrote:

Dear Mother,

We beat Battersea 4–1!

I'm always the last to be picked. Ian and I went to Alvaro's in the King's Road last night to supper and we went in Ian's Rolls-Royce! Ian, all scruffy 'cos he says if you dress smart in that kinda car you are in danger of looking like your own chauffeur! You can hear him saying it, can't you?

Guess who was in Alvaro's? Princess Margaret! Halfway through our meal, I went to the loo and had a good look at HRH Princess M. She gave me a cross look for staring and I said, please forgive me for staring, your Royal Highness, but tomorrow is the day I must write to my mother and she will never forgive me if I don't say exactly what you are wearing. Black dress, sleeveless with a black lacy bolero jacket over, and pearls.

There's a theatre play in the offing and a good film for next year, so everything in the garden is coming up roses and daffodils. Ian and I are planning to go to Edinburgh to see Tom in *Hamlet* . . . hope Dad's on good form, and see you soon,

love, Rodney.

I sat in bed with Albert, weighing a ton on my legs, and read through the letter thinking how she'll like the bit about Princess Margaret, and rather proud of the lace bolero jacket. I enjoyed reading the letter and I thought about turning it into a script for a comedy. You see a bloke like me, writing letters to his mother, tends to gild the lily somewhat.

What to call him/me? Albert Courtenay? No, I'll drop the 'e' in the middle of Courtenay, just in case Tom says anything. And the series shall be called – *Dear Mother . . . Love Albert*.

Things had cooled between Daphne and me and I was besotted with Paula, very young, very pretty, and very well connected. We drove to Devon in the white Porsche to meet her mother, who didn't approve on sight and made me feel like a dirty old man. Well, Paula was very young and I was twenty-six, well, all right, more like nearly thirty – OK, thirty.

I was writing *Dear Mother . . . Love Albert* when Patti Boyd, Paula's sister, rang to say she wanted to see me. In fact, she said she *must* see me. Oh dear! Half an hour later, I opened the door and there was George Harrison on my doorstep! They both looked grave. George stared at me and said, 'Oh no, not you!'

I asked them in and sat them down in the living-room. I told them I'd go and put the kettle on. When I came back they looked even more stern. Patti spoke first. 'Now look, Rodney. You must know why we are here. Paula's only seventeen, just out of school, it's not er . . . suitable. That's all . . . my kid sister, for God's sake!'

George looked distinctly uncomfortable.

'You two were together a long time before you got married,' I said. 'It's common knowledge.'

Then in that doleful Liverpool drawl, he said, 'Yeah, but that's got nothin' to do with why we're here.'

I tried to lighten the atmosphere. 'Are you saying it's all right for a Beatle and not a Likely Lad?'

They just sat there.

'Would you like a cup of tea, won't take a minute?'

'No, thank you.'

'No.'

As they got up to leave, I mentioned how much I liked the Beatles' latest single 'Love is all you need'.

Paula and I went out to dinner that night to San Lorenzo's, Beauchamp Place with Ian and Fiona and Cathy McGowan who presented *Ready Steady Go*.

I asked Cathy about me and Paula and she said she thought Paula was a bit young. 'She is awfully young. I thought you were going out with Daphne, from Grumbles? I liked her.'

I was intrigued. It was the Swinging Sixties, wasn't it? The permissive society. Yet Paula's youth shocked people.

I found Paula a flat to silence all the flak about her being so young.

My parents came to stay. My mother and I made such a dinner, and then we waited for Paula to come. We waited and waited but no Paula. 'I'm just going out, Mum, won't be a minute.' Across the New King's Road, up Lettice Street and Mimosa Street. Paula opened the door with such a strange look on her face. We went upstairs, me very cross.

'You know my parents are down from . . . why didn't you ring if you can't face . . . posh meal all ready . . .'

I pushed my way into her room, and there on the bed was a young boy. I know him, I thought, he's the member of a group called 'Grapefruit', or is it 'Marmalade'? And he was lying on Paula's bed, his back resting against the wall, very much at home. Paula went and sat beside him. I thought, I've been jilted for a grapefruit segment.

'Are you coming to meet my parents? Dinner – you said you'd be there straight from . . .'

'No.'

'Oh right, right then, what'll I say . . .?'

'Tell them what you like.'

'Look, I'm going . . . are you coming?'

'No.'

We left the room, I was shaking, Paula was shaking. Down the stairs, and Paula opened the front door and outside on the doorstep and that's when I hit her.

I didn't know I had hit her until it was in the past. I had never hit anyone before, and I never have since, certainly not a girl, a young girl. I slapped her face, only once and very hard. It must have hurt. I walked away, back home to my parents. I was still shaking, thinking, oh I wish I hadn't hit her.

My parents and I had dinner. It wasn't a very jolly meal.

Late that night, when everybody was in bed, I heard someone banging on the door. I went downstairs, pulling on my royal blue towelling dressing-gown. On the doorstep stood Colin, Paula's elder brother, furious, and he pushed past me. 'You hit my kid sister. No one hits my sister!'

Into the living-room.

'Right, right, you've got some good stuff here, sound stuff and pictures and that. I'm going to smash them all then I'm going to smash you!'

'Look, Colin, let me go upstairs and put some trousers on, will you? No one is going to beat me up without my trousers on, OK?'

Upstairs on the landing, outside her bedroom door, my mother stood in her nightie and with strange things in her hair. 'What is it, Rodney? What's the matter, I heard . . .?'

'It's all right, Mum, you go back to bed. It's just Colin, Paula's brother, come round to beat me up.'

'Right! Just let me put my teeth in. I'll talk to him.'

I'll never forget the scene in my living-room, my mother's arms outstretched, holding both Colin's hands in hers, looking him straight in the eyes, very emotional, both of them.

'Now see here, Colin, we are just ordinary folk!'

Well, no one could beat me up after that.

I almost felt sorry for Colin. He dropped his shoulders and left without another word. We heard the front door close behind him. My father came into the room. 'What's up, Bessie? I heard . . .?'

'It's over now, Horace. You go and put the kettle on.'

And I lay awake that night and wished I hadn't met Paula, hadn't been such a fool.

I rang Philip Jones, the boss of Light Entertainment at Thames Television. I knew he was a big fan of *The Likely Lads*. I told him I'd had an idea for a comedy series. 'Come to lunch.' That's more like it, I thought.

At Thames, by the river at Teddington, Philip Jones and I walked into the executive dining room and we bumped into Benny Hill, who asked me if I couldn't get rid of Jimmy Bolam. 'You and me, Rodney, would be much better. He's holding you back.'

At lunch, Philip asked what kind of character Albert Coutney was. I said, 'Oh, he's like me. You know, gauche, naive, clumsy . . .' When I said clumsy, I put down my wineglass, the stem broke and a whole glassful flowed into Philip's lap. 'Oh, do a pilot!' he said.

I had a date with Celia Johnson. I took Celia to the ballet at Stratford-upon-Avon. We had supper after the ballet at the Dirty Duck, and all the ballet folk were enchanted with Celia and, I think, vice versa. Then we drove back to her home, Merrimoles House, just outside Henley, where I was to spend the weekend working on the script for Thames Television.

The house had been designed by Celia's husband, Colonel Peter Fleming. The setting amongst beech woods was stunning, with a great long vista cut behind the house, stretching for miles and miles and miles.

I could see immediately that the colonel regarded me as an oddity. 'One of *her* friends.' I found I had a gift for putting up minor 'blacks' with him. People called him Colonel, or Sir. He was very sticky.

He asked me how I was.

'Oh, you know, grey! It's a dull, grey day, and I feel grey and dull too. You know, down. Down and dull and, er, grey!' I looked at him. His eyebrow was raised and he muttered, 'Oh dear.'

I was supposed to say, 'Fine, I'm fine,' and leave it at that.

Celia had told me he would go off shooting in his beech woods every day, his pipe in his mouth and his dogs at his heels. Naturally, I patted and stroked one of the dogs as soon as I saw it. 'Don't do that!' he bellowed. 'They're gun dogs. One only pats them as a reward for bringing game back.'

'Oh, sorry, I didn't . . .'

Before dinner the colonel gave me two bottles of wine to put in front of the fire of the drawing-room to breathe, ready for supper. He had drawn the corks and shoved them back in the bottles. I did as I was told, and carried on talking to Kate and Lucy, their daughters. Later the colonel came in to collect the bottles. 'Oh dear, he's left the corks in!' he said, to the fireplace, but of course everyone looked at me.

They played an after-dinner game called Bang-bang CABBAGE! Someone taps twice on the table or a plate with a teaspoon, and on the third tap you have to say something with a connection to what someone's said before . . . like. Tap tap Apple, tap tap Tree, tap tap Sap! You had to be quick.

The Fleming folk were awfully good at the tap-tap game, as I would get slower, and I was always the first to lose three lives. One evening, Celia, in charge of tapping, in her best *Brief Encounter* voice started with . . .

'Church.'

Tap, tap.

'Steeple.'

Tap, tap.

'Vestry.'

Tap, tap.

'Vestments.'

Tap, tap.

'Vicar.'

And the beautiful Kate, the elder of the Fleming children, whose turn it was before me:

Tap, tap.

'Bishop.'

Me – loudly,

Tap, tap. 'PRICK!'

The colonel said, 'Oh dear.'

Celia said, 'Prick, dear? After Bishop?'

I gushed 'Bishopric? Like when you become a Bishop . . . awarded the Bishopric of the dio . . . Oh, heck . . .'

The colonel said, 'Shall we change the game?'

The pilot of *Dear Mother . . . Love Albert* went well and I had a meeting with Philip Jones the following week. I was very nervous. Philip said he would like to see a script for Episode Two and a synopsis for a further four if we were to go to series. I opened my bag and slid a script across the desk towards him. 'Episode Two, Philip, oh, and here's some pages of where we thought we would go if we did another four to make it six.'

Philip laughed . . . then: 'And what about studio time? Would July and August suit?'

I was in a film of a stage play, Bill Naughton's *Spring and Port Wine*. Also in the cast were James Mason, with Diana Coupland as his wife, Susan George and Hannah Gordon, Frank Windsor and Avril Elgar. We went to a very exotic location in the north – Bolton, Lancashire, and there we found a Mrs Rodgers' house at the end of a row of Forties houses, high above the town with a view down into the valley, a view of factory chimneys and mill buildings . . . perfect. Mrs Rodgers opened the front door in her pinny.

'Yes?'

'Good morning, my name is Peter Hammond, and I'm sure you know this young man. We are going to make an international feature film up here with James Mason in it and we would like to use the front garden of your house and the side with the wonderful view down into Bolton . . .?'

'Oh come in, come in, oh, I don't believe it . . . James Mason. Come in, you're not leaving this house without a cup of tea and a Marie Louise biscuit! Oh, I do wish Len was home from the mill, he's never about when . . . now, sit down and I'll go and put the kettle on . . . James Mason!'

She guided us to two comfy armchairs in the front room. 'I've just had a terrible thought.' I've gone *ashen*! 'How many people will come up here when you start the film, the film proper, like?'

'Oh, perhaps thirty or forty, or so, it's quite a big unit.'

'Oh no . . . no, I knew something would happen to spoil it, I've only got eight cups!'

Daphne and I were together again. We drove to Stratford to stay with Michael Williams. The night of Apollo 11, standing in Michael's garden and looking up at the moon I thought, one small step . . . imagining a man walking on the moon, and I asked her to marry me.

She said, 'I think I'd still keep my flat on.' By this time she had a full-time job at Biba, a store in Kensington Church Street. The owner, Barbara Hulanicki, had started the business with a little boutique in Abingdon Road, selling 'a gingham shift and scarf at 25 shillings, see mail order catalogue'. Now there was a move to Kensington High Street and Daphne was Miss Black, the buyer, and happy in a world of design and colour.

Biba was a Mecca to all the dolly birds; they went to Biba first, then the King's Road. Barbara Hulanicki, who I thought very beautiful, thought herself big-boned and had devised a 'look'. She cut the arm hole so high up the body that the torso looked long and skinny.

At Biba's Kensington Church Street shop, Julie Christie stripped off to her knickers like all the other girls, trying on clothes. She was looking for clothes for the film *Darling*. Cathy McGowan and Cilla Black were regulars and Mrs Frank Sinatra (Mia Farrow) came with Samantha Eggar. Yoko Ono left with a dress, which she cut up on television that evening, and Mick Jagger brought Marianne Faithfull. One day Barbara said with a huge wink: 'Should see who we've got down to her knickers in the corridor!' She opened the door of her office the smallest crack and there was Brigitte Bardot.

I can't give this, oh so brief, account of Biba without mentioning suede boots! Oh yes, you can, says the editor, because I'm cutting it out! (Has he? We'll see, as grown-ups say.) Those suede boots – purple, grape, plum, mauve, dusty pink, deco green, mulberry and bluebottle and Biba brown, knee-high with a zip up the inside, tight of course, and with a three-inch heel; Barbara said: 'Daphne told me she thought I had gone too far.' I still think of those boots.

I was busy casting all my friends in *Dear Mother . . . Love Albert*. I now had a co-writer – Derick Goodwin. We did great in the ratings: Episode One was in at number five, then eight, ten, six, ten, five – and that's a hit. We were asked to do a 'special' for Christmas Day.

Philip Jones asked me to go and see him while we were making the Christmas special. He sat me down and gave me a drink. 'We are not going to do a second series, lovey. Now, don't look like that.' He explained how full the studios were with shows already booked for the following year. 'You are a success, you *should* do a second series . . .' I did have the sense to realise how good this was of him, since he could easily have done it through agents. I had the relatives down to the recording of our Christmas show: Auntie Elsie and

Auntie Edna, and they were all photographed for the *TV Times* having Christmas lunch in November.

I went to a lunchtime reception at the Mayfair Hotel. Donald Baverstock, boss of Yorkshire Television at the time, told me he loved *Dear Mother . . . Love Albert*.

I said, 'Oh, would you like it?'

'Beg pardon . . . how d'you mean?'

'Would you like it at Yorkshire Television?'

'Yes, I would. Is it yours, er . . . to give?'

'Yes.'

'Then my answer would be yes. We would like it at YTV. Thank you very much, boy.

I couldn't wait to get out of the building and get to a phone. When I did, I rang Philip Jones at Thames Television. 'Philip, it's Rodney, listen. Donald Baverstock says he would have it at YTV. *Dear Mother . . .*, I mean, Can I? Is it mine to give? What do you think?'

'It *is*, and you *can*. I'm sorry to lose you and we wish you all the best.'

Chapter 18

I SPENT TWO YEARS at Yorkshire Television. I had to ban my mother from the studio audience at Leeds. I found it strangely off-putting to see her in the front row, turning around and telling everyone she was my mother, and worse, quietly crying with pride.

I loathed *No Sex, Please, We're British* when I read it, I thought it cheap and rude and common. Did I have an overblown opinion of my own worth? Yes, I did.

For God's sake, who was I worried about seeing it? Tom? Jimmy Bolam? I turned down a play that made its leading man a star. Michael Crawford went on to become a national treasure, and that play, though it found little favour with the critics, ran and ran.

I also turned down *Confessions of a Window Cleaner*. That would have made me a great deal of money, too, but I think it would have changed my life in the wrong way. It was a time of great decision-making.

On one of our regular trips to the north Ian La Frenais and I made a detour to see my Auntie Elsie. Ian parked the Rolls-Royce outside the little grey semi-detached council house. They were all there, my mother, Auntie Margaret, Auntie Edna and Auntie Elsie. I asked her, 'How's me Uncle Jim?'

'Finished!'

'Oh . . . I am sorry.' Poor Uncle Jim, he had always been chesty.

'Aye, he hasn't got the breath and he can't march!' By breath she meant the brass band. 'And Lancaster's that uphill and all cobbles,' she continued.

'Mind you, Elsie, I don't think Dunkirk did him any good.' This from my mother. 'Standing in all that water, waiting for a boat!'

When it was time to go, Ian was kissed goodbye by all the aunts too. We climbed into the Rolls and Ian was silent for a long time. Eventually he said, 'Ee Rodney, your Auntie Elsie!'

'I know, I know.'

Driving back, Ian suddenly asked me. 'What do you think about doing *The Likely Lads* again?'

'What?'

'You heard. I've been thinking about it, mentioned it to Dick . . . like to call it *Whatever Happened to . . .*'

'Oh, Ian, that's terrible. *Whatever Happened to the Likely Lads?* S'n open invitation to the critics, that! You can't be serious?'

I told you I was never good at titles.

But even then, in the car, I knew in the back of my mind that Dick and Ian had been confident that I would be a pushover. It was James Bolam who would be the hard one to persuade. They took him out to lunch. 'We made him laugh so much, telling him what we had in mind, by the end of the lunch we had him hooked.'

April, May and June, and *Dear Mother . . . Love Albert* was still doing well in the ratings. What would I be giving up? I wouldn't be producer, co-writer and main actor in my own series any more. I would be giving up all of that to do a sequel to something I had done six years ago. Would it be goodbye to Albert Courtnay? He had been very good to me, bought me my first Bentley and a house in Cornwall, but more than that I had a niche at Yorkshire Television. It meant a lot to turn my back on all this.

I thought I must consider this carefully, I must think long and hard. No, I didn't, not really.

We all met up at a lunch in Alvaro's, in the King's Road, hosted by Duncan Wood from the BBC. Duncan beaming, thrilled the Corporation were going to make the series. He went back a long way, having directed Hancock, and was now Head of Comedy. He raised his glass.

'Here's to *The Likely Lads* back again, Rodney and Jimmy, Ian and Dick!'

Jimmy said, albeit with a tough grin, 'Hang on, hang on. I haven't seen all the scripts yet. No one shits on me!'

Good start, wasn't it? Dick, the great diplomat, launched into how Jimmy had laughed at the script outlines, and the first two bottles of wine went down fast, but I shall never forget the look on Duncan Wood's tired, old veteran face.

Thelma had first been mentioned way back in *Rocker* in 1966. '*Gerraway! You've always had a thing about Thelma Chambers ever since Park Juniors . . . you gave her your Plasticine!*'

And now, here Thelma was, in Jimmy Gilbert's office. As Dick explained to actress Brigit Forsyth what Thelma was like and the more he and Ian described what they were looking for, the more right Brigit looked. Ian says in the book about *Whatever Happened to The Likely Lads?* by Richard Webber: 'We all loved Brigit and, though she was ideal for the part, we could have written the character as one-dimensional but tried our hardest not to. She could easily have been disliked and seen as the obvious, archetypal threat to the boys, but Brigit managed to change that and create a character of her own. Thelma may be bossy, but she's not a snob: she's just a likeable good person, with an understandable point of view as regards Terry.'

Episode Two. *Storm in a Tea Chest*

(Terry HELPS Bob MOVE HIS BELONGINGS INTO HIS NEW HOUSE, BUT Thelma DOESN'T WANT THE 'USELESS REMNANTS OF HIS PAST' IN THEIR NEW HOME. Terry PERSUADES HIM TO TAKE A STAND, SO HE TELEPHONES Thelma FROM THE PUB TO TELL HER.)

BOB:	(RETURNING TO PUB TABLE) I didn't need these. (GIVES Terry SOME COINS)
TERRY:	Oh aye, short call, was it?
BOB:	To the point.
TERRY:	What did you say?
BOB:	I said I was not prepared to give up my heritage, that it's my home as well as her home and where those things go, I go.
TERRY:	Well put. What did she say?
BOB:	She gave me one of her ominous silences.
TERRY:	So what did you do?
BOB:	I gave her one of my ominous silences.
TERRY:	Pretty pointless phone call really then, wasn't it?
BOB:	It made its point, it made its point, then the pips went.

Perhaps Brigit got more of a look-in than Sheila Fearn as Terry's sister, but Sheila was very popular too. I meet men now who still say, thirty years on, 'Oh, that Terry's sister! She was the one I had my fantasy about . . .!' or 'I would imagine being on a date with Terry's sister . . . well, you couldn't with Thelma, could you? She was so er . . .?'

'Aloof?'

'Unobtainable?'

'Hmm . . . that too.'

The first episode of *Whatever Happened to the Likely Lads?* had a lot going for it. Dick says the first three scripts flowed fast.

Episode One. *Strangers on a Train*

(Bob STEPS INTO Terry's TRAIN COMPARTMENT AS THE LIGHTS FAIL. HE'S BEEN TO LONDON TO BUY Thelma A WEDDING PRESENT, A BAROMETER.)

BOB: Sod it . . . sorry. Was that your foot?

TERRY: I've got another one.

BOB: Power cut.

TERRY: Typical.

BOB: Would you believe it? 1972. The jet age, high-speed gas and all that "Inter-City makes the going great". Huh.

TERRY: Typical of this country.

BOB: That'll mean no heat as well. Any heat your side?

(THERE IS A PAUSE WHILE THE SOUND OF SCUFFING IS HEARD IN THE DARK.)

BOB: Oh, sorry . . . again . . .

TERRY: It was my knee that time.

BOB: Sorry, mate . . .

TERRY: How far you going?

BOB: Newcastle.

TERRY: Well, sit down, will you? Or I'll be black and
            blue by the time we get there.

BOB: You live up that way?

TERRY: Near there. Haven't been back for ages. Just
            come out of the army.

BOB: Oh aye. Enjoy it?

TERRY: Got a lot out of it, got a lot out of it.

BOB: I nearly went in once.

TERRY: Could have done a lot worse.

BOB: Funny story attached to it, really. You see I had
            this mate; my best mate, you know, really close.
            And anyway, few years back, I decided to go into
            the services. You know – get away for a bit, see
            something of the world. So I signed on. Well,
            when I went away, this mate of mine couldn't
            take it. Went to pieces. Couldn't function with-
            out me. I suppose it was like losing your right
            arm. So he signs on too. Just to be with me. Only
            you'd never guess.

(THERE WAS A PAUSE WHILE Bob's LAUGHTER IS
HEARD IN THE DARK.)

BOB: (CONT.) He gets in and I get discharged. Flat
            feet! So I'm free again and he's lumbered for

three years. You should've seen the look on his face. I still laugh when I think of it. I mean it's a sad story in some ways 'cos he's never spoken to me since. But when you're telling the story, like when you're telling someone else you do see the funny side. I mean you've got to laugh.

(Bob HAS GOT TO LAUGH AGAIN. WHEN HE STOPS THERE IS A SILENCE. A LONG SILENCE. THEN:)

TERRY: You bastard!

(SUDDENLY THE LIGHTS GO ON. AFTER FIVE YEARS Bob AND Terry ARE TOGETHER AGAIN, FACE TO FACE. Bob IS AGHAST, AS IF HE'D SEEN MARLEY'S GHOST; AND SPEECHLESS. NOT SO Terry.)

TERRY: (CONT.) You bastard. You've got to laugh, haven't you? You've got to see the funny side of it? You've got to laugh at the fact that your best mate missed the most important years of his life. It's a JOKE. While you were back home enjoying the Permissive Society, I was in every god-forsaken corner of the globe sweating my bollocks off. Got to laugh at that . . . I missed it all! Swinging Britain was just hearsay to me. Something I read about in the overseas edition of the *Daily Mail*. The death of censorship, the new morality. Oh, Calcutta, topless waitresses and see-through knickers.

BOB: They never caught on, topless waitresses, I mean.

So, dear gentle reader, that's how the *Likely Lads* met again after five years. I must just mention another page I remember from that first brilliant script.

BOB: I saw your mother the other week. She looked very well.

TERRY: Oh aye.

BOB: Not to speak to like, just through the car window.

TERRY: Through the what?

BOB: The car window.

TERRY: What car window?

BOB: My car window.

TERRY: You've got a car?

BOB: Well, I haven't just got the window.

It's the simple things that amuse me, I laugh at that . . . NOW. Important plot in that episode, further into the script.

BOB: If you'd kept in touch . . .

TERRY: I meant to, Bob. When I came back that first Christmas, I fully intended to make it up and wipe the slate clean. Then me Mam told me you'd got engaged to Thelma Chambers . . . so you know . . .

BOB: You never liked Thelma, did you?

TERRY: Course I did! That's got nothing to do with it. It was just that bit about realising that nothing's going to be the same again; you can't turn the clock back. Just brought me down that's all.

Nothing to do with Thelma. I admire her. Always have.

BOB: We broke it off just after that.

TERRY: Did you?

BOB: Yeah.

(THERE IS A PAUSE WHILE Terry THINKS, THEN PLUNGES IN.)

TERRY: Well, I can't say I'm sorry. To be perfectly honest, Bob, that's a load off my mind. I can say it now. 'Cos I mean, you are my mate and if you're going to get married, get married, but not to Thelma Chambers, you can do better than that.

(Bob's EXPRESSION HAS CHANGED TO STONE, BUT Terry IS OBLIVIOUS TO THIS.)

TERRY: (CONT.) I never could see what you saw in her. She didn't half have airs about herself. She was so stuck up she thought her arse was a scent factory. What's the matter?

BOB: I am marrying Thelma in six weeks' time.

TERRY: But you said . . .

BOB: We made it up again.

(THIS IS IN THE BUFFET CAR ON THE TRAIN WHERE THE LADS HAVE BEEN DRINKING BEER (REAL) AND SMOKING. Bob LEAVES IN A GIANT HUFF AND Terry, AFTER A MOMENT GETS UP AND

GOES TO THE BAR. The Steward LOOKS AT HIM QUESTIONINGLY.)

TERRY: Same again . . . no, hang on. I'll have a short. Scotch
           . . . I sacrificed the best four years of my life for that
           fella. And now he tells me he's getting married.

(The Steward PUTS A COMFORTING HAND ON Terry's.)

STEWARD: Never mind, sailor. Lots of other pebbles on the
           beach.

Bob about to marry Thelma, and Terry Collier back as just cause and many impediments. If that isn't enough grounds for a thirteen-week sequel to the *Likely Lads*, I don't know what is!

The Likely Lads was mostly longish duologues between the two lads, and thirteen half-hours was six and a half hours of television, individually both parts longer than *Hamlet*.

Daphne had been to Turkey, Italy, Germany and France, and now while I was filming she went to India with Barbara Hulanicki. Barbara searched for goodies for the store, and Daphne looked for cloth.

Then with work over, they hired a car to see the sights. Their driver had shown George Harrison and Patti Boyd the sights and insisted on taking Daphne and Barbara on the same magical mystery tour. At one temple near Bombay, famed for an enormous fertility symbol standing proudly at its centre, they were told to walk round it, and that if they perhaps touched it, this would lead to very positive results. Apparently Daphne just kept on walking around it and touching it and stroking it and patting it . . .

Episode Two: *Home is the Hero*

(EXTERNAL HOUSING ESTATE FILM DAY. BOB'S
NEW HOUSE, HIGHFIELD'S ESTATE, KILLINGWORTH,
NEWCASTLE UPON TYNE. NO. 8 AGINCOURT.)
(Bob, THE PROUD OWNER (THOUGH HE AND Thelma
HAVEN'T MOVED IN YET) STEPS BACK AND
INDICATES.)

BOB: There she is.

TERRY: Looks a canny house though, but . . .

BOB: We haven't got a name yet.

TERRY: You'll need one, won't you, or you'll never find
            it again.

BOB: What d'you mean?

TERRY: Well, look at it – they're all the same aren't they?
            Rows of 'em.

BOB: No, no, these are quite different. Our living-
            room's sixteen by twelve. They're fifteen by
            thirteen down there.

TERRY: I must be blind.

(INTERIOR BOB'S NEW HOUSE. STUDIO DAY.)
(Bob AND Terry COME DOWN THE BARE WOODEN
STAIRS AND THEN INTO THE LIVING-ROOM. THIS
IS CARPETED AND THERE IS EVIDENCE THAT Bob
HAS BEEN PUTTING UP SHELVES. A NEW SOFA IS
PUSHED AGAINST THE WALL. A SERVING HATCH
LEADS THROUGH TO THE KITCHEN BEYOND. Terry
LOOKS AROUND.)

BOB: Under-floor central heating – we've decided to be all electric. Lots of points – well-made jobs aren't they?

TERRY: Is that wall plumb?

(Terry IS LOOKING ALONG ONE WALL, HIS HEAD ON ONE SIDE.)

BOB: What? Course it is, what makes you think it isn't?

TERRY: Nothing. Just that I have an instinct for things like that. Nasty cracks in that plaster.

BOB: That's just settlement. Always get a bit of that. Bound to be a few teething troubles. Like having a new car.

TERRY: Had trouble with that as well?

BOB: No, I haven't had trouble with that as well . . . apart from the starter motor.

TERRY: There's something so depressing about these estates. Just the thought of you all, waking up at the same time, all eating the same low-calorie breakfast cereal, all coming home at half past six, switching on the same programme at the same time and having it off the same two nights a week.

BOB: Look, we haven't had a chance to personalise it yet. Once everyone moves in and chooses their own decorating and their own curtains. Got a flair for things like that, has Thelma. We're having mauve and seaweed green.

TERRY: Least that's unusual.

BOB: We were having yellow, but they're having that next door.

TERRY: Aye, well, that's my point, isn't it? You've said it all.

(Terry WALKS TO THE WINDOW AND LOOKS OUT ON TO THE STREET.)

TERRY: (CONT.) Just seems sad to me. When you realise the only way people can tell the difference between you and everyone else . . . is the colour of your curtains.

BOB: So what's wrong with being the same as everyone else? What's wrong with trying to make some modest progress. I've worked hard the last four years, and I've got this to show for it, and the car. Mightn't mean much to the Burtons, but it means a lot to me. So what's so special about your life style? You're homeless, car-less and single – what does that amount to? Terry Collier, Bachelor Pedestrian.

(SURPRISINGLY, Terry DOESN'T REACT TO THIS IN HIS NORMAL HOSTILE FASHION. INSTEAD HE LOOKS AT Bob FOR A MOMENT, THEN WALKS AWAY, HURT.)

BOB: (CONT.) Oh, I'm sorry, that wasn't a very nice thing to say.

(NO RESPONSE FROM Terry.)

BOB: (CONT.) Stupid anyhow, why should you be

interested in all this? Fellow like you. Doesn't want to be lumbered with a wife and a mortgage. That's not your scene. Can you imagine *you* married? With all those birds out there. All the good times to be had. I was always the one falling in love all over the place. But not you. You were cool. Kept your head. Safety in numbers. You're a born bachelor. Aren't you?

TERRY: Aye, you're right.

BOB: Naturally independent.

TERRY: True, true.

BOB: There you are, then.

TERRY: Only one problem.

BOB: What?

TERRY: I'm married.

BOB: Pardon?

TERRY: I'm married. I–am–a–married–man!

(Bob IS INCREDULOUS. ALSO SPEECHLESS. HE STARES AT Terry FOR SEVERAL LONG MOMENTS.)

TERRY: (CONT.) Say something, then.

(STILL NOTHING.)

TERRY: (CONT.) Haven't you got anything to say?

BOB: Have you got a bottle opener?

(Terry IS PUZZLED AND CROSS.)

TERRY: Why?

BOB: I've got some brown ale in the kitchen. I need a
           drink.

(INTERIOR THE SAME (LATER) DAY)
THE BOYS ARE SITTING ON THE FLOOR. Bob IS
POURING BROWN ALE INTO CUPS.

BOB: Right. Now, start at the beginning. Don't skip
           around. Tell it from the start. I want it all.

TERRY: Listen, Bob, this is the story of my marriage.

BOB: It's the story of the century, mate. It's so . . .
           unreal. It's like me getting a life peerage, or
           Darlington winning promotion.

TERRY: I'm glad you're getting so much fun out of it,
           Bob. Perhaps you'd like to ask your mates around
           and you can all pee yourselves at my misfortune.

BOB: Misfortune?

TERRY: Wounds are deep. Scars haven't yet healed.

BOB: I'm sorry . . . I didn't realise . . .

TERRY: I've only just learnt to live with the pain.

BOB: Oh, forget it . . . I mean don't talk about it . . . if
           it hurts too much. You mustn't feel you have to
           tell it all. Just give us the recorded highlights.

TERRY: It's not *Match of the Day*, you know . . . you can't
           wait can you?

BOB: Sorry, sorry. In your own time.

(Bob GIVES A DISINTERESTED SHRUG, AND TAKES A
SWIG OF BEER. Terry GETS TO HIS FEET.)

TERRY: During my military career, two things happened to me which have left an imprint on me for the rest of my life. The first was when I got pissed in Hamburg one night and got tattooed on my left buttock.

(Bob IS INCREDULOUS.)

TERRY: (CONT.) The second, was a rainy day in November '69 when Jutta Paurngarten, spinster of München Gladbach, and I got married.

BOB: Incredible.

TERRY: Fact.

BOB: Was she . . .?

TERRY: Funnily enough, she wasn't.

BOB: Rich dad?

TERRY: Not especially. Had a few pfennigs put aside, but nothing much.

Bob, INCREDULOUSLY REACHES THE LAST ALTERNATIVE.

BOB: Love?

TERRY: (ANNOYED) That's your last alternative, is it? She's not pregnant; she's not loaded, so this must be love.

You've just read this scene, but you can't hear the pauses. Or perhaps you can? I waited an age before saying 'Was she . . .?' and then 'Rich dad?' and again 'Love?' After the recording we all went out to supper to Pontevecchio in the Brompton Road, at a big round table, this was to become a ritual 'do' after recording an episode.

Later that night, I was in bed and heard the phone ringing. Two o'clock. It was Dick Clement.

'I just wanted to say thank you, er, thank you for those pauses. Memorable. Well done. Spot on. I know it's late but I wanted to congratulate you.'

'Night, Dick . . . n'thanks.' I was thrilled. He must have been thinking about that scene as he was going to bed. It was nice of Dick and it was typical of him.

Episode Seven: *No Hiding Place*

(THE LADS WANT TO AVOID HEARING THE RESULT OF A FOOTBALL MATCH BETWEEN ENGLAND AND BULGARIA TO ENJOY WATCHING IT ON TELEVISION THAT EVENING . . . THEY HAVE EIGHT HOURS BEFORE THEY CAN SIT DOWN, RELAX AND WATCH THE MATCH. THIS IS THE SHOW MOST REPEATED, THOUGH THERE ARE OTHERS AS CLEVER, AS FUNNY. THEY FIND 'SANCTUARY' IN A CHURCH IN THEIR SEARCH TO AVOID NEWS MEDIA, NO RADIO, TELEVISION, AND NEWSAGENTS' PLACARDS IN A CHURCH, BORED.)

TERRY:	I spy with my little eye, something beginning with . . . F.
BOB:	(INSTANTLY) Font.
TERRY:	How did you get that? Right then. I spy with my little eye, something beginning with . . . S.G.W.
BOB:	Stained glass window.
TERRY:	Oh, well, that was an easy one. Any fool . . . right . . . right.

Terry IS NOW IRRITABLY DETERMINED. HIS EYES
LIGHT ON A BIBLE ON A LECTERN.

TERRY: (CONT.) I spy with my little eye, something
            beginning with . . . B.
BOB: What?
TERRY: B.
BOB: Sorry, I thought you said P. B, is it? Oh, Bible.

(Terry IS FURIOUS. HE RESORTS TO LYING, BUT HIS
MOMENT'S HESITATION HAS GIVEN HIM AWAY.)

TERRY: Wrong.
BOB: Why did you hesitate? It is Bible, isn't it?
TERRY: No, it isn't.
BOB: (sly) Oh, all right, then I give up. If it's not Bible,
            what is it?
TERRY: Pardon?
BOB: You heard me, come on, what is it? Quickly,
            quickly.

(Terry's EYES SCAN THE CHURCH DESPERATELY
FOR ANOTHER B.)

TERRY: Well, if you want to give up . . . it's not Bible, it
            never was Bible . . . if you're giving up . . .
BOB: Cheat.
TERRY: Who is? It's . . . it's . . .

(SUDDEN INSPIRATION.)

TERRY:	(CONT.) It's Belfry!
BOB:	Belfry? The belfry's the tower up the top. Nobody's little eye can spy the belfry from here. I mean who am I playing with? Superman with his X-ray vision? I thought it was for people with normal eyesight. I didn't know it was 'I spy with my little X-ray eye'.
TERRY:	I didn't know the belfry was in the tower. I thought the belfry was that little room over there.
BOB:	*That* is the vestry.
TERRY:	How am I supposed to know that? What chance have I got playing with an ex-choirboy.
BOB:	I spy with . . .
TERRY:	Oh, I'm sick of that . . . what time is it?

I guess I loved that scene because it was so childish, James and I so comfortable with each other. We got on very well in those days, though the press always wanted us to be sworn enemies.

I asked Eric Morecambe about this and he told me it was the same with him and Ern. He explained that if you don't get on it's a double page spread in the *Daily Mail* and follow-up pages in the Sundays, but if you tell them you had dinner together the night before it doesn't even make a sentence.

'Tell 'em you go to bed together!' he said

'You what? . . . I can't . . .!'

'Well, you did! That night before you married Thelma . . . I saw you! S'a good 'un, that.'

'Oh, I see . . .'

'I do! I tell 'em, I wouldn't go to bed with Ern, 'n lie there while he's writing his plays, if we didn't get on!'

166

At our big round table at Pontevecchio's Jimmy was always very funny. Daphne adored his acerbic wit. He was with Sue Jameson, who had been in *Double Date* (Episode Two *The Likely Lads*) in 1964. Around the table were Ian and Fiona, Dick and Jenny, Mike Hugg, and Linda. Mike was ex-Manfred Mann and the composer of the theme songs for *Dear Mother . . . Love Albert* and *Whatever Happened to the Likely Lads*, who famously ever only says, 'Hmm.'

Jimmy was holding forth about unions. 'Like, I mean, the Variety Artists Federation, the Electricians and Technicians Unions . . . if there was solidarity . . . there'd have been no commercial telly strike like.' And here he thought to include Mike. 'F'instance, Mike, you're in a union . . . the Musicians Union.'

'Hmm.'

'Yes, well, you're obviously not the spokesman for them!'

A peculiar thing happened to Jimmy in the studio at the end of the recording of *No Hiding Place*. We had succeeded avoiding that football result all through the day and evening now, the last scene, we came through the door into the living-room of Bob's new house. He said, 'Right, we've made it, let's just sit down, relax and *m*atch the *w*atch.'

I played a few more lines then stopped with a shrug of my shoulders and a grin. 'Sorry, my fault,' I said. 'Can we go out and come in again?'

Jimmy gave me a look 'What did you do?' and we went off the set to start the scene again. I thought, Why tell him what he had said? He obviously had no idea. The floor manager idented the scene and 5-4-3-2 Cue and we came through the door again, and Jimmy said, 'Right, we've made it. Let's sit down, relax and match the watch.'

He had said the same thing again, and some of the audience picked up on it this time. Again I played another couple of lines, then stopped, making out I was unhappy about something. We came in again and the same thing happened. Outside the doorway now, I told him.

'Jim, you're saying "Let's sit down and match the watch".'

'Never . . . no?'

'Yeah, truly.'

'Shit.'

'Doesn't matter, come on.'

'Scene Nine, Take Four and 5-4-3-2 Cue.

We came through the door and Jim said the line correctly, but he opened a bottle of Newcastle Brown Ale and it erupted like Vesuvius all over the coffee table.

'And cut!'

We did Take Five and a second bottle of beer erupted like the first one, having stood too long under the hot lights. So we were into Take Six, coming through the door again and now through gritted teeth:

TERRY: Right, we've made it! Let's sit down, relax and
           watch the match!

At last, with flat beer poured back into the bottles, we managed to get to the end of the show. Jimmy was cross with himself and showed it, although it really didn't matter. He didn't come to the bar afterwards or to Pontevecchio.

The following Tuesday morning at the rehearsal rooms, at the read-through for Episode Eight, *Guess Who's Coming to Dinner?*, Jimmy sat slumped in his chair in a sulk and mumbled through the script semi-audibly. This was baffling to the people guesting in that week's episode, Julian Holloway (Stanley Holloway's son) and the busty Jacquie-Ann Carr.

Jimmy's attitude that morning seemed even worse, perhaps, as Dick and Ian were there. We were lucky to have them at read-throughs, because afterwards they would go to the canteen and rewrite any pages that needed it. Of course, Julian and Jacquie-Ann had no idea why Jimmy was in such a black mood.

Perhaps they thought he was always like that? I wondered if he was taking it out on me. Perhaps he hated the fact that I'd been cool and in control? But there were many times he'd helped me out when I had forgotten what on earth was coming next, dried up, stone dead . . . it was inexplicable . . . unfathomable.

We had a code, sort of, in the early days of 1964 – I would say 'mind you' and Jimmy would say 'still' if we weren't sure what was coming next. It might have been the other way around . . . you can go on saying 'still' and 'mind you' for ages!

TERRY: See you Friday, then?
BOB: Friday? Oh, yeah. But still . . .?
TERRY: The Fat Ox? Lads' night?
BOB: Oh, yeah . . . mind you . . . er
TERRY: Still . . .?

That meant we neither of us had any idea what was next.

That Friday night the audience was coming in and the huffiness of the read-through was forgotten. I seem to remember we started on a bit of a nervy level, but *Guess Who's Coming to Dinner?* is one of my favourites, possibly because it's a bit about snobbery.

(Bob AND Thelma TAKE Terry TO A DINNER PARTY WITH Alan AND Brenda. AND Thelma ACTUALLY DEFENDS Terry.)

(INTERIOR ALAN'S HOUSE. STUDIO NIGHT.)

ALAN: Oh, I think I hear the girls coming down. You
            know my wife, Brenda, don't you, Terry?

TERRY: Brenda? No, I don't think so.

BOB: Yes you do. *Brenda!*

TERRY: I don't know any Brendas.

(ENTER THE Girls. Terry LOOKS AT Brenda WITH
INSTANT RECOGNITION.)

TERRY: (CONT.) Oh *that* Brenda.

BRENDA: Hello, Bob. Hello, Terry. How nice to see you
            again.

(IT OBVIOUSLY ISN'T. SHE GIVES Terry A RATHER
LIMP HANDSHAKE.)

BOB: Yes, well, isn't this nice. Reunion. After all these
            years . . . isn't this nice? Takes you back to Park
            Juniors Four B, doesn't it . . . isn't this nice?

BRENDA: I'd like to think we've come a long way since
            Park Juniors.

TERRY: *You* certainly have, Brenda. When I first knew
            you, you were living above your dad's chip shop
            near the glue factory.

ALAN: Did your father have a chip shop, darling?

TERRY: A good 'un an' all, The Silver Grid. Big helpings
            an' all with free batter.

BRENDA: (FROSTILY) I'd better see how things are
            doing. Would you give me a hand, Alan?

ALAN: Sure, love.

(THEY LEAVE. WHEN THE DOOR HAS SHUT.)

THELMA: You'll never win any prizes for tact, will you,
          Terry?

TERRY: What d'you mean?

BOB: Look, Terry, some things Brenda doesn't want to
          be reminded about. You know she's always been
          a bit . . . a bit . . .

TERRY: Stuck up?

BOB: There's nothing odd about someone who gets
          older, gets a bit of money, gets a nice home,
          wanting to forget the past. There's no harm in
          someone who lived above a chip shop wanting to
          batter themselves – I mean better themselves.

TERRY: My lips are sealed.

(THE MEAL IS SERVED.)

THELMA: Do we have a fondue set on our wedding list?

BOB: We will have tomorrow.

THELMA: What lovely table mats. These are new.

BOB: Ooh, hunting scenes.

BRENDA: I just haven't had them out before. They were a
          present from Aunt Elsie.

(Terry FORGOT HIS LIPS WERE SEALED WITH FOND
MEMORY.)

TERRY: Oh, yer Auntie Elsie. How is she, Brenda? Is she
           still a cleaner at the brewery?

(INTERIOR THE SAME (LATER) NIGHT.)

BRENDA: Should we move from the table?

TERRY: Aye well. I'll pop upstairs and er . . . wash me
           hands.

ALAN: First on the left. Light's above your head.

(Terry LEAVES, THE OTHERS MOVE OVER TO THE
FIREPLACE AND SETTLE THEMSELVES.)

BRENDA: Shall we leave the past. I find our days at Park
           Juniors very irrelevant. I have some memories
           that aren't so pleasant.

THELMA: Oh, you mean the boiler room incident.

BOB: What's this?

BRENDA: Do we have to?

THELMA: You were full of it at the time.

BRENDA: It was most upsetting. I was attacked by two boys
           in the pitch dark of the boiler room. If it hadn't
           been for . . . been for the janitor . . .

(SHE SHUDDERS AT THE MEMORY. Terry RE-ENTERS.)

TERRY: Hey, Bob . . . I've just been thinking . . . What
           was the name of the girl who seduced me and
           you in the boiler room?

BRENDA: How dare you!

TERRY: What?

ALAN:	Oh, come on love, it was years ago.
BRENDA:	It's monstrous – I was attacked.
TERRY:	Where's this?
BRENDA:	In the boiler room.
TERRY:	So were Bob and I. If it hadn't been for that janitor . . .
BOB:	Isn't this fun . . . happy days . . . memory lane.

(BUT Brenda's 'BOTTLE' HAS GONE AND SHE LAUNCHES INTO Terry.

BRENDA: Part of your reluctance to leave the past, Terry Collier, is that you have very little to look forward to in the future. And your present has little to offer beyond the pub and the billiard hall. Most of us have improved ourselves, developed as people. But you're an embarrassment to your family and an embarrassment to your friends.

BOB: He doesn't embarrass me. He might be coarse and he might be vulgar . . .

TERRY: Are you with me or against me?

BOB: Shut up a minute. He might be crude and he might be rough at the edges. And all right he might have eaten the wrong end of his asparagus. But I'll tell you one thing . . . he's down to earth and he's honest.

BRENDA: Well! Here's a turn up for the book! The good old days again. Those two back in the saddle.

(SHE LOOKS TO Thelma FOR SUPPORT, BUT GETS NONE.)

THELMA:	I think Bob's right.
BRENDA:	What? I never thought I'd see the day when you took Terry Collier's side.
ALAN:	I like a lively discussion.
THELMA:	Terry is honest. And that's something we all seemed to have lost since Park Juniors. He's got no pretensions. He would never deny that he lived above a chip shop.
TERRY:	(TO Alan) I didn't live above a chip shop.
BRENDA:	What are you trying to infer, Thelma. That I'm a snob?
THELMA:	Yes, you are, Brenda. You're an enormous snob. You always have been.
BRENDA:	What a bitchy thing to say.
THELMA:	But it's the truth.
ALAN:	I like a frank exchange of views.
BRENDA:	If I was such a snob, why would I invite *that* into my house for dinner.
THELMA:	I'll tell you why you asked Terry. Because the only way you can measure how far you've come from 23 Dog Lead Lane is to parade your possessions in front of an audience. I've seen you do it before. You watch people admiring your fabrics, and praising your carpets and envying your Peter Jones fondue set . . . and you cream your drawers!

You must forgive me quoting pages, but I've only picked out five or six scenes from thirteen episodes . . . and they are my favourites.

Episode Three: *Cold Feet*

Bob's WEDDING IS APPROACHING AND HE TELLS Terry HOW HE'S FANCIED Thelma SINCE EARLY SCHOOLDAYS.

BOB: When she went to grammar school I became her social inferior.

TERRY: In our school we were everyone's social inferior.

BOB: I used to watch her through the railings, skipping, her blouse tucked into her thick navy blue knickers. As Paul Anka put it at the time: 'So near, and yet so far away'.

TERRY: Billy Fury!

Jimmy Gilbert, our producer, objected strongly to 'thick navy blue knickers'. Perhaps it was a Scottish thing? He said, 'Look, I've got a daughter, and er . . .' We overruled him. The speech wasn't just about knickers, was it?

The last episode in that series of *Whatever Happened to . . .* was called *The End of an Era*. It was our thirty-fourth counting the early black and white ones.

Bob's wedding to Thelma Chambers happens at last. The lads are getting ready:

BOB: What was your honeymoon like?

TERRY: A time of great distress.

BOB: What did you do?

TERRY: We went down the Rhine on a barge. We went on a barge, down the Rhine. Or up the Rhine, I don't know which it was. I do know it was full of Germans, in their braces, playing the accordion. And she had a sore throat and she gave it to me and it was pissing down, and we rammed a jetty.

And then later in the church what did we talk about waiting for the wedding march to herald Thelma's progress down the aisle?

BOB: What time is it?

TERRY: What time does your watch say?

BOB: A quarter to three.

TERRY: It's a quarter to three then.

BOB: We're early.

TERRY: Of course we're early. That's because we left home early and drove here too quickly. Could have had another cup of tea and watched the two-thirty from Chepstow.

(IN THE BACKGROUND THE CHURCH IS FILLING UP. Bob LOOKS AT HIS WATCH.)

TERRY: When did you put that plaster on?

BOB: Just after I said goodbye to the cat.

TERRY: My cousin got scratched by a cat and his arm swelled up to twice its normal size. Apparently some cats carry this fatal infection. Just an ordinary cat it was. Much like your Justin. Should've had a tetanus injection on the way here. We had enough time.

BOB: Give us your hanky, will you?

TERRY: What for?

BOB: I want to blow my nose. I think me hay fever's
           coming back.

(Terry TAKES OUT A HANDKERCHIEF.)

TERRY: Hang on, hang on.

(HE EXTRACTS A PIECE OF CHEWING GUM FROM IT
WHICH HE STICKS TO THE UNDERSIDE OF THE
PEW. Bob BLOWS HIS NOSE AND DABS HIS EYES. HE
TAKES OFF HIS BUTTONHOLE FLOWER.)

BOB: Take yours off, it's the pollen.

TERRY: Probably a symptom of the dreaded cat infection.

BOB: I must have an allergy.

TERRY: Maybe you're allergic to getting married. Maybe
           you'll spend the rest of your married life sniffing
           and sneezing and snivelling. And the only cure
           will be divorce.

(Bob SNIFFS IN REPLY. Mrs Ferris AND Aunt Beattie TAKE
THEIR PLACES BEHIND THE BOYS.)

TERRY: You can get a very quick divorce in Mexico. I
           think you just have to live there two weeks.
           Mind you, some countries you just have to stay
           the weekend. I think in Guatemala you just have
           to apply by letter. You just drop them a line with
           a five-pound postal order.

BOB: Surely that only means you're divorced in Guatemala. Which isn't much help if you're living on the Elm Lodge Housing Estate.

(Mrs Ferris WHISPERS TO Aunt Beattie.)

MRS FERRIS: What are they talking about?

BEATTIE: Divorce.

MRS FERRIS: Oh.

TERRY: Unless, of course, you went to live there. Residence they call it. But I can't see that. Not with your hay fever and your terror of spiders.

BOB: Do they have nasty spiders in Guatemala?

TERRY: Terrifying. Apparently . . . they can devour a guinea pig in a minute.

BOB: Why? I mean, why a guinea pig?

TERRY: What? Well, it just happens that a minute is the time it takes them to eat a guinea pig. Something like a fox terrier probably takes a bit longer . . .

BOB: Oh.

TERRY: Apparently . . . in Colombia, beyond the far uncharted reaches of the Amazon, lives the deadliest animal in the world. It's not a spider, and it's not a snake. It's . . .

Wait for it, wait for it . . .

         the great venomous toad. An ounce of whose poison could wipe out the whole of West Hartlepool.

BOB: They've got enough trouble with their beer.

TERRY: Talking of great venomous toads, Thelma's mother's arrived.

Chapter 19

I WENT OUT TO dinner with Rod Steiger and Tom and Cheryl.

Tom had met Cheryl Kennedy in an Alan Ayckbourne play. They had kissed in the play and that was that. He was smitten. Cheryl Kennedy is one of these clever girls who can sing, dance and act, but there was a daughter, Sam, and a husband, 'Dave the builder', so it was all a bit fraught. Tom likes peace and heavy quiet on his sofa with Schubert. He likes to be alone.

Rod was on great form at this dinner. He would pretend to be tough, but he was really a pussycat.

I took Rod to Queen's Park Rangers football club. It was the era when Rodney Marsh was their big star, and as we came down the long steps between all the rows of seats the chant went up:

'Rodney! Rodney! Rodney!'

Perhaps fifteen to twenty thousand fans were chanting. Rod Steiger waved back, a big magnanimous wave that a South American dictator would be proud of, as we continued down the steps, acknowledging every side.

'Rodney! Rodney! Rodney!'

★

Tom hired a cook. He was filming long hours and the thought of a decent meal at the end of the day and not having to cook or go out to restaurants was very attractive. Zena was very short and very round, a Michelin girl. One night I went round to see Tom, and Zena opened the door. She said, 'Where were you Monday night? Tom said you were coming to dinner, and no Rodney.'

'Monday night? . . . Oh, I wasn't asked, didn't know anything about it.'

'Tom said you were coming and I made steak and kidney pie, and Tom asked for extra chips because you were coming.'

It seemed extraordinary what he had to do to get extra chips!

Zena's other great claim to fame, apart from cooking for Tom, was that she was featured nude on the famous album cover, Jimi Hendrix's *Electric Ladyland*.

I was on tour when I read in the papers that Tom and Cheryl had got married – I was shocked. It was all over the papers and I hadn't been asked, I didn't even know about it. I felt very miffed as we'd been friends for twelve years.

I watched the first episode of *Whatever Happened to the Likely Lads?* in my little Cornish cottage. Show business and career and all suddenly seemed such a long way away.

Later I was in the pub with my fishing friends Plugger, Pedro and Bunny Legge. I go crabbing with them and fish and help haul the pots.

Plugger asked me, 'What's next, Bewesey?'

'Oh, dunno, Pluggs, tide's gone out a bit.'

'You come along with us, Spider B (my nickname). Pedro and me are going on a big crabber up Looe with the Mad Monk from Mullion. There's a fourth berth.'

After some weeks at Looe, Baggy, brother to Niblo, top fisherman there, took me aside. 'Now, see here, er, Spider B, we got yer now, boy, you're right on. You don't like going on about being on no television, you pull your weight and accordin' to the Mad Monk you're right on in a boat too . . . but.'

Here we go, I thought.

'I gotta give you some criticism about *The Likely Lads*!'

Oh dear, now for it.

'There's not enough cunt in it!'

February gales make our days hard but exciting; I'm never seasick and feel no fear. The fishermen respect the sea and the weather forecast is compulsory listening . . . I feel safe with Pedro and Plugger and the Monk.

In years to come I often thought perhaps I should have been putting myself about more in London, meeting people, being seen, but the year before I'd done seven episodes of *Albert* which I had co-written, produced and starred in and sang the song, and then thirteen episodes of *Whatever Happened to . . .?*

Now I was happy to be a beastly fisherman.

One weekend I was excited because Daphne was coming down. I walked up the hill to No. 1 Chapel Terrace to ask Plugger's dad if he fancied a trip to Redruth Station to meet her. Everyone calls him 'Old Man', though he's not yet fifty.

'The London train's delayed an hour, possibly an hour and a half,' I said, 'we'd best go into the club.'

'Right on, come on, Bewesey.'

The club? It was an asbestos hut the other side of the iron bridge at the end of platform one, with 'The Railwaymen's Club Affiliated' on the illuminated sign. As we entered, 'Hello, Old Man, all right?'

The train was delayed another half hour then another. Some time well past midnight, I heard it finally arrive. I ran out of the Club Affiliated and hared up the long platform. I saw Daphne leaning out of her carriage door, looking lovely, smiling.

But her smile faded as she saw me, bright red in the face after weeks at sea, and I don't expect the donkey jacket and short wellies helped. And then what did I say? To my smart fashion-buyer girlfriend I hadn't seen for ages . . . and I probably said it in broad Cornish too . . . 'All right, boy?'

She gave me a look, and if I could have read her mind it would have said . . . What am I doing here? What did I ever see in . . .? When is the next train back?

'Give us your bag, we're having a drink in the club hut.'

At the long bar, Old Man asked, 'What'll it be, Daf?'

'Three whiskies, please.'

'Three?'

'Three, in a line in front of me, please!'

When we left to go home, the VW convertible refused to start. Old Man and I were pushing it down the steep hills of Redruth, Daphne sitting in the back with the hood down surrounded by her bags, looking uninvolved. She had needed another three whiskies before we left the Railwaymen's Club Affiliated.

'The same again, in a line in front of me, please!'

To get over the shock of seeing me.

My father died. I heard the news off the Eddystone Light. I collected a dark suit and headed north. After the funeral I took everyone to a country club, a sort of Edwardian pile. The uncles thought it was wonderful that all the drinks were on a tab.

Very soon the compliments flew. What a good man Horace was, what a gent. Well, he was a good man, a very gentle man.

I remembered asking when I was a little lad, proper, proper poorly, 'I say, Mum, did you really love my Dad when you got married, like?'

'Well, Rodney, he was a lovely dancer.'

I remembered how he enjoyed going to Blackpool or Bournemouth for NALGO, his union, with Albert Northrop and George Blood.

And I recalled the time I took him and my mother to a smart restaurant in Chelsea, and how he was intrigued to see Twiggy there. Afterward, in my house in Fulham, he said, 'So that was Twiggy, was it?'

'Twiggy?' said my mother. 'Where? I never saw Twiggy! Was she in't restaurant? Oh, Horace, why didn't you say? Well, I am upset – typical!'

But I had noticed he never took his eyes off her, sitting at a table opposite.

'She had on this, er, shirt dress, I think you'd call it,' he told my mother. 'Black shiny and silky wi' long rounded . . . er, lapels, like. And round her neck those strings o' black beads like Whitby jet, shiny too, and round her head a red and white spotty hankie, you know like a pirate . . . not that . . . ah . . . noticed, Bessie.'

Suddenly, standing in that country club with my mother, my uncles and my aunts, I felt I had to ring Daphne.

'How's it going?'

'Oh sad . . . you know.'

'Yes, I know . . .'

'Oh . . . let's get married straightaway.'

'Silly . . . are you sure about getting . . .?'

'Yes, I'm sure, go to Fulham Register Office on Monday on your way to work and ask if we can do it next Saturday, will you?'

'Yes . . . goodbye, Rodney.'

'Yes, goodbye, Daphne, oh . . . er, and lots o' love!'

'Lots o' love, bye.'

So there we were, on Saturday, 24th February at Fulham Register Office just down the road from Stamford Bridge, the home of Chelsea football club, the venue of our first date. Outside, the pavement was packed with journalists and photographers and news cameras.

It was a fine sunny day and Tom and Ian and I looked so funny and serious in the photographs. The ceremony in the register office was lovely and fun, because of the lady who conducted it. Everyone laughed, and I wished my father had been there. Ian took everyone to lunch at The White Elephant, and – typical Ian – the cake bore the legend 'Shop-girl marries TV Star'.

In the afternoon, Daphne and I went home to Bettridge Road, expecting everyone to follow us for champagne . . . but nobody came. They all thought, mistakenly, that we would want to be alone . . . we didn't, and were very disappointed.

'What on earth shall we do, all afternoon?' Daphne said.

We got up to watch ourselves coming out of Fulham Register Office on the television news.

On Monday morning, Daphne went back to Biba and I went back to Cornwall to my fishing boat and Plugger, Pedro and the Mad Monk.

We were planning a joint honeymoon with Tom and Cheryl, to Marrakesh. A mistake, as it turned out.

Chapter 20

W^{E'RE LEAVING ON} a jet plane . . . don't know when I'll be back again . . . well, I do actually – in two weeks' time. Daphne and me and Tom Courtenay and Cheryl off on our honeymoon together. There was also Cheryl's four-year-old daughter Sam, and Cheryl brought her mum and dad as well. Rick was a trombone player in a band and Joy was a soubrette. I think the plan was that they would look after Sam while the two attractive young couples holding hands went sightseeing. It didn't work out like that, because Tom was happy by the hotel pool with a good book, by himself, if the truth were known – and he didn't want to leave the hotel.

The pattern was set on the plane. There was someone we knew, George Layton and his wife Vera. George was in the first series of *The Likely Lads* in 1965, and Vera is fun and gets on immediately with Daf and Cheryl. We have a party on the plane, Daf, Cheryl, George and Vera and I. The parents look after Sam, and Tom's into a book.

On the second morning, Tom wandered into our bedroom at the hotel and seemed to be fascinated by our breakfast tray.

'No, er . . . how did you get that?'

'Rung up . . . just rung up, er, room service.'

'Oh, I see. Just like that?'

Tom had been abroad a lot, Spain, Paris and Hollywood, but on films where the first assistant, or the second assistant, or the third assistant director looks after the star's every whim. It's part of their job description. Tom was naïve about looking after himself, or pretended to be.

I found a wonderful place to go out to supper, Maison Arab. George and Vee were up for it and then I asked Tom and Cheryl. Cheryl was mad keen to come, but Tom wasn't. 'Oh . . . you mean go out? Er, leave the hotel . . . won't it be a bit late, er . . . I think we'll stay in. There's Sam, you know.'

Daphne and I, beginning to think it's a good job we've got George and Vera with us, piled into a taxi. We were driven through a maze of back streets until the driver told us he could get no nearer, and we would have to walk. I had a map from the hotel and directions from the taxi driver. We found Maison Arab with some degree of difficulty.

There were cool, tiled courtyards with fountains playing. The guests sat cross-legged on cushions around the walls at low Moroccan tables, eating with their hands. Near midnight Cheryl suddenly arrived.

'Oh, I couldn't resist it, what a wonderful place!'

'But what have you done with Tom?'

'Oh, you know Tom. I just said I'm going.'

'But . . . but how did you get here?'

'Taxi, you know . . . then I had to walk, this very nice Arab boy showed me the way.'

Cheryl, a blonde, pretty English girl, all alone, had walked through the souk, the market place, and down narrow alleys to find us. She could've been . . . well, anything could've happened.

'Cheryl, you could've been sold into white slavery.'

'Goody! I'm walking back then, all right?'

'No, you're not.'

Near the end of our idyllic honeymoon I hired a car. Tom just couldn't get over it.

'You've done what? . . . How did you do that?'

'You just go up to the desk in reception, the one with the Hertz sign and you ask to hire a car.'

With the help of Fodor I had planned a journey up the Atlas mountains. The guide book suggested where to stop for morning coffee and where to take luncheon and '. . . from this point it is barely twenty kilometres to the summit and a splendid, memorable view of the Sahara Desert laid out before you in one vast panorama'.

'But . . . no? What kind of car?'

'A Peugeot, does the make matter?'

'No, but *outside* Marrakesh . . . up a mountain? Rodney, are you sure about this?'

We set off early the next morning. The most beautiful blue sky above, and a lovely day, quite a holiday atmosphere in the car, Daphne beside me in the front, Tom and Cheryl in the back. Not far out of Marrakesh, we travelled on a high dusty road, one side a wall of rock the other a steep drop to a distant valley floor with a river snaking through. And perched high up the other side of the valley was a Berber village, flat-roofed houses of red mud, one on top of the other, clinging to the peaks in the hot sunshine.

'Stop, stop the car, I must take a picture of that.'

'Why? Why are we stopping? Daphne, you're not getting out?'

I joined Daphne about a hundred yards behind the car down the road, Daphne started taking photographs of the Berber village. Tom came running from the car, running fast.

'Quick, quick! They're coming.'

I looked to see . . . what? Camels, racing at full tilt, carrying the Tuareg tribesmen riding hard, their long rifles held high? No, it was a group of children begging, village urchins calling out for pennies . . . and I don't think they were armed.

'Quick, get in the car . . . start the engine.'

I did as I was told. I couldn't risk a glance at Daf or Cheryl. Tom opened his window and threw a shower of coins out as we drove away. In my wing mirror I could see the children scrabbling in the dust.

'That was close!'

We stopped a lot higher up at a café for wonderful thick powdery coffee, then on, up and up to the place Fodor had suggested for luncheon. We ate outside under sail-like awnings and drank lovely cool wine. Afterwards, I drove on, but thinking about what Fodor had said of that view of the Sahara.

Tom said, 'No, I really think we should turn back. We've seen enough, haven't we? I mean what time will we get back? We'll have missed the er . . . is this wise? Are you sure of the way, Rodney?'

What was it the guide book said? '. . . from this point it is barely twenty kilometres to the summit and a splendid, memorable view of the Sahara Desert laid out before you in one vast panorama'!

'No, I mean, do you really know how far it is from here?'

I didn't.

'What if a mist comes down . . . a storm. The Mistral . . . a desert storm? A sand storm . . . the Sirocco, is it called? Can make men mad!'

He had his way. I turned around and headed back to Marrakesh. I could feel the girls furious with me for giving in. Down we went past the lovely place where we had had lunch, then past the coffee place and then there, on our left this time, that high Berber village, and we never saw the Sahara Desert laid out before me in one great vast panorama.

In Cornwall, after the honeymoon, I was being a beastly fisherman again and plodding up the hill in thigh boots.

'Now, Rodney,' said my neighbour Rene Jane, 'your agent's been on the phone. A film in Spain, *The Three Musketeers*. They want you for three days.'

I pulled a face. 'Oh, I don't suppose it'll be much. I think I'd prefer to go fishing.'

You must imagine this in the kitchen of a thatched and ancient cottage and in a thick West Country accent.

'There's Michael York in it 'n' Oliver Reed and Charlton Heston . . . oh, and Raquel Welch! Now then, I must get this right . . . your part is a Shifty Spy!'

'Oh, Rene, I'm really not that bothered, you know. I like my life on the old *Mez Creis* with Plugger and Pedro. I don't need it.'

Now Rene looks stern. 'Rodney, you *go*! It's your job.'

'Oh, Rene . . . I really think . . . I mean, how good a part is it? . . . A Shifty Spy?'

Now it's Daphne's turn. 'Rodney, it's better than "*second* Shifty Spy"!'

Chapter 21

DAPHNE AND I went to see a gynaecologist. The big front door of the Harley Street House premises opened and we climbed to the marble halls above. The grand circular staircase rose to a domed glass lantern skylight with the sunshine streaming through. Gynaecologist Michael Cameron was tall in his three-piece suit, thumbs in waistcoat. While I sat at his desk he took Daphne into a corner and behind a screen examined her.

I kept wanting to cry (Daphne appalled).

Then going down the staircase afterwards, Daphne said, with emphasis, 'I can't have a baby in front of that man.'

'Why?'

'He's far too dishy.'

'Oh.'

I went to 'father's night' where all the prospective dads sat on the floor with cushions for pregnant tummies, very embarrassed at having to groan and pant and do quick gasping breathy sounds.

'Now, you all want to know what it's going to be like for little wifey, don't you?'

None of us did. We all wanted to be somewhere else.

★

Daphne had her things packed. She was to have something called an epidural, and the baby would be induced on Saturday morning, and I was getting organised. In Daphne's room now, I laid out smoked salmon and sliced rye bread, lemon and black pepper. I'd brought champagne from home, and tins of Guinness, to make Black Velvet, were chilling in one of the clinic's fridges.

Michael Cameron came in to see me, his eyes taking in the champagne and Guinness, the smoked salmon on rye, etc. The only thing missing is perhaps paper hats. And he did look very dishy in his green loose cotton jacket and trousers and white rubber shoes.

I had a little girl, I was terribly thrilled and thought it a miracle . . . and I was the only dad in the world. Daisy came into the world at 1.40pm and weighed six pounds and fifteen ounces. She was very beautiful and looked so content and peaceful, sleeping in the crèche along the corridor.

Daphne was livid. The nurses wanted her to sleep, but she said: 'Look, I don't want to sleep, I want to have a party and ask people over and drink champagne and Guinness, and bet on the horses, and . . .'

I wasn't to have any say in choosing the name. Daphne chose it like she and Barbara choose things for Biba, and it was just right.

'Why Daisy Jay?'

'No particular reason, really.'

'Come off it, you were reading *The Great Gatsby* in the clinic.'

'No really, they are just nice names.'

She will contradict me. Never agrees with what I say!

In the lifts and in the canteen queue Eric Morecambe and I have a double act – two camp old character actors.

'Darling! Wonderful to see you, isn't that whatsisname over there? Absolutely dire in *Doctor Finlay's Casebook*.'

'No, that's David Vine, dear. Did you see *The Brothers* last night? Now I am surprised they brought *that* back.'

'You here tomorrow? I must bring my address book and get your number, you're not still with . . .?'

The canteen manager took me aside one day. It seemed we had upset someone, there had been complaints, he said. 'Someone in *The Brothers*?'

I noticed he didn't tell Eric Morecambe off though.

The next morning. 'Oooh look, is that Dandy Nichols? Sitting next to that bloke in *Colditz*, pity they ever let him out, dear.'

And there was that canteen manager looking at me.

I promise not to mention all thirteen scripts of the second series of *Whatever Happened to . . .?* But I just want to mention this because it was so typical of the writing and those twists of plot that made it so special. In the second episode, Bob and Thelma return from their skiing honeymoon and, of course, Bob has a leg in plaster. He tells Terry. 'I did not do this skiing!'

'I warned you about a skiing honeymoon, I warned you!'

'I did not do this skiing.'

On the plane home, the newly-weds had to suffer extreme turbulence and Bob, feeling giddy, had fallen down the aircraft steps.

Then in Episode Twenty, Bob had a leg in plaster again after he and the dreaded Thelma had been on another skiing holiday, this time in the Cairngorms. While they were away Terry had done some much-needed odd jobs about Bob's new house in return for being allowed to stay there. Thelma, looking around the living-room, thinks she's been harsh in her recent assessment of Terry until, because of his shoddy workmanship, Bob's leg comes crashing through the ceiling, dropping the centre light on her head.

Bob then has to go to hospital to have his plaster fixed, and the hospital porter is Terry, pushing a wheelchair for Bob. He has been forced to take the job because his dole has run out. Faster and faster down an incline.

In Episode Twenty-One, *Affairs and Relations*, Bob and Terry go away on a fishing weekend. Bob, riddled with guilt, is forever ringing Thelma from the hotel. It turns out that this is the same hotel that Thelma's father is staying at with his secretary when they are supposed to be in Edinburgh at a trade fair. Thelma's dad was played by Bill Owen, who was to go on to become a national treasure in *Last of the Summer Wine*.

Then Thelma decides to come up and join Bob.

Terry is getting on fine with the sexy barmaid.

Thelma's in bed in Bob's room when the door slowly opens. In the darkness, the barmaid enters in her nightie. Then enter secretary, also in her nightie. Thelma leaps out of bed to reveal a short nightie. Bob protests they have both come to see Terry. In the corridor Thelma pulls open Terry's bedroom door and we see Terry in bed with, yes, you've guessed it, Thelma's father. It was a script Feydeau would have been proud of.

We spent Christmas in Cornwall. Daphne and the nanny and the cat and Daisy, aged three months and nine days. Then I'm back up north, filming. Bob Moncur asked me to a New Year's party. I had known Bob and his wife Camille since the early days of the *The Likely Lads*. Bob was captain of Newcastle United and Scotland. I asked Jimmy Bolam if he wanted to come. 'They're canny folk though,' I said.

'What? People I don't know! I should hate it. A house full of people I don't know, all enjoying themselves. Bloody suburban people in their bloody suburban home.'

'Fine, fine. OK. If you change your mind, I'm off at about half seven.'

'I won't change my mind!'

As I was leaving the hotel, there suddenly beside me was the angry Bolam, wrapped up warm in his overcoat. 'Yeah, well, I just thought I'd come, all right?'

'Fine, fine, lovely.'

Bob Moncur came to drive us to the party, and Jimmy had the most fabulous time.

I was sent out before midnight to 'First Foot' the house, and before we left we had Gaelic coffees and I showed them all photos of Daisy. 'Now, this is Daisy Dot in a leopard skin outfit from Biba, this one is . . .'

Bobby insisted on driving us home. Jimmy in the back had his arms around Moncur's neck as he was driving. They were now bosom buddies.

The next morning when he came down to breakfast: 'Hey what lovely people! Great night, eh! I love Bobby! What a great guy. I don't remember coming home, I don't remember. How did we get home?'

'Your mate, Bobby, drove us.'

'I don't remember. I just don't remember!'

There is to be a *Whatever Happened to . . .?* Christmas special. The story so far: Bob and Thelma are dressed as Captain Hook and Peter Pan. Brigit in a very short Peter Pan outfit, complete with pixie cap . . . oh, oh, oh. The minicab arrives to take them to a fancy-dress party. The driver is none other than an angry Terry Collier. Terry stays on at the party, Bob goes missing. Too much cheap red wine and he's got the red mist and is off with Sylvia Braithwaite. Thelma asks Terry to drive her home. Someone has taken his minicab and the police are called. In the last scene, in Bob and Thelma's new house, the policeman says the cab has been found, no damage and a man was seen running away from the scene. A witness said the man couldn't really be described in the darkness, but he did notice a large gold earring. Bob comes downstairs and joins the group . . . he is wearing a dressing-gown and his pyjamas, no trace of the Captain Hook outfit except . . . what's that dangling from his left ear?

THE END

When we were doing the night shoots in Newcastle for the Christmas special, it was freezing cold, so we went into a pub for a warm up. I was dressed as Captain Hook, three-cornered hat with white plumes, leather thigh boots, long red frock coat and a sword and those gold earrings. I sat next to this lady on a bench along a wall. She said, unimpressed, 'Ah thought Halloween was ages ago!'

Now I never attempted a Geordie accent in *The Likely Lads*, I spoke like I normally speak. We always thought my native Yorkshire near enough.

'But I do know who you are,' she continued.

'Oh, aye?'

'I love your Geordie accent.'

'Oh aye? What is it you like about it?'

'I know what you're doing.'

'Oh aye, what am I doing, like?'

'You're doing POSH Geordie!'

*

Daphne and I made another journey to Harley Street. She was in a black mood. It seemed it was all my fault. Michael Cameron was still looking dishy but Daphne wasn't at all happy. As soon as he came through the door, she said, 'It's *his* fault!'

'Ah, do sit down,' said Michael.

'He hid the pills!' she said.

'I see . . . and how is, er, Daisy?' said Michael.

I don't think I did hide the pills, though I did think it might be nice to have a little friend for Daisy. 'When do you think it'll be . . .?' I said.

'Oh, early days, possibly around Christmas time?'

'Ah, another Christmas special! Ha, ha!'

'Sorry?'

'Shut up, Rodney.'

I had a telephone call out of the blue from Nat Cohen. Now I had seen Nat Cohen step out of his Rolls NAT 1 in Wardour Street, a dapper little man with trademark moustache like a stage army major. I had also sat next to him on the top table at a Variety Club lunch. So many British films begin with a Charles Atlas man holding up a globe and those white letters circling it saying 'Nat Cohen and Stuart Levy Present'. And now Nat Cohen was ringing me. 'Rodney! At last we have the finance in place to do a film of *The Lively Boys*!'

'Oh, I see . . . er, that's, er, wonderful.'

'That's right, it is. Now I want us to have lunch.'

'Today?'

'No, not today . . . next week, Thursday?'

'Oh, I can't that Thursday, I've got a dental, erm, that day, er, can I ring you?'

'No, don't ring me, I'll ring you. Ha, ha!'

But he did. 'Rodney, Nat Cohen . . . what about the Gay Hussar? You'll like the Gay Hussar.'

And I put him off again. I put him off three times. I would have loved to have lunch with Nat Cohen but I thought we needed a script, a Clement and La Frenais script, but they were very, very busy, three thousand miles away.

It was time for me to go to Hollywood.

The newspapers found out I was going to Hollywood, and a lot of them assumed I was off for good.

'LIKELY LAD QUITS OUR SHORES FOR HOLLYWOOD.' There were a lot of press photographers at the airport.

In the evening, when we arrived, Ian met us and drove us in his Rolls-Royce to BelAir, a very exclusive area where the houses are all mansions with security gates. He pressed the window button. Swish. I took a deep breath.

'Can you smell it? Can you smell it, Rodney?'

'Hmm, yeah, and I know what it is. It's eucalyptus. Eucalyptus trees!' I'm pleased with myself.

'No, Rodney, it's money, that's what it is. MONEY!'

A few days later there was a party, but Daphne was all Hollywooded out and decided not to go.

It was the most fabulous party I had ever been to. Everyone was asked outside for 'cabaret time'. It was getting dark and everybody sat facing the step up to the pool. Along the edge of the pool were coloured candles in glass pots. Then people got up and did a party piece – but what people!

Milton Berle introduced the first 'turn'. Anne Bancroft sang in close harmony with a lady I didn't know. They sang three songs to get everyone in the mood (I should mention that there was a small orchestra playing the accompaniment). Then it was Mel Brooks's turn. He sang two songs, a parody of Sinatra. Then he and Anne Bancroft did a scene from a film: he was Jerry Lewis. It was hysterical.

Then Mel Brooks asked me why I hadn't done anything and I heard myself say, 'Huh, me? I used to know this Scottish monologue, a guy used to do it in full Scottish regalia when I was in the RAF.'

So I did it.

'Wee Davie said, "Can I no go and fechkt alongside the Phillipstines?"'

No one was laughing. I could see Ian trying to signal to me to stop, but I was too far into it. Mel and Anne just looked uncomprehending. Ian McShane was signalling too. When I finished they all smiled politely.

I will never laugh about this to this day. It is something to wake up and go red in the face about.

Rod Steiger said, 'Come to lunch on Monday, Rodney. I am filming, so come and see how we make movies in Hollywood.'

I wondered if I should go. When you are not a part of it you can be awfully spare.

I turned up at the set and I had never seen so many trailers and vehicles, film location equipment and stuff, cables snaking under a big black heavy curtain. I slipped through and was right behind the camera. The camera was pointing at WC Fields.

'And CUT! That's a print.'

The director turned from the camera and said, 'Hello Rodney, how are you? Arthur Hiller. We met in London, Rodney.'

'Oh, right!'

Then Rod came over in full WC Fields make-up and costume. 'Goddam you, Rodney! You turn up just in time for LUUUNCH! I'll have to take yeeerh. Come with meeee!'

We climbed into the longest, blackest limousine and we were driving down Beverley Boulevard.

'Where you wanna go, boy?'

'Oh, Rod, I don't know, er, it's your town like, I don't . . .'

'Arnold? Pull in over there. The Four in Hand looks a fine place to have lunch with my friend from London.'

He *was* WC Fields.

'Arnold, when you have moored this barouche you are required to join us for lunch.'

'Than' you, sir.'

Rod's make-up had taken two hours, a wonderful WC Fields nose and a red hairpiece, and he was wearing striped trousers and white spats and carrying white gloves. The maître d' was holding the biggest menu you've ever seen.

'Maître d'? I didn't book. I would like a table, a quiet table in a corner. This is Rodney, my friend from London.'

The maître d', leading the way, was totally unfazed as if this was an everyday occurrence. 'This way, Mr Steiger.'

No one in the restaurant bothered us. Arnold, the driver, joined us for lunch. We had Caesar Salad and lovely Californian Chardonnay. Rod drank water, the only thing out of character with WC Fields.

We went to the MGM Grand, Las Vegas. We have the best seats in the house. The lights go down. I don't know it but I'm about to see the greatest show on earth! The chorus line is seventy long and from the ceiling descends topless, seven-foot tall girls of all colours and nationalities, with exotic plumes of many colours and nationalities too. The scene changes were like film merges: we saw a trolley bus *Meet Me in St Louis* clang, clang, and then we merged to an African safari with elephants and camels, and we saw Siegfried and Roy with tigers and black panthers.

It was the most spectacular show of our lives, but I wanted to get Daphne back to our hotel room. I kept thinking of the mirror on the ceiling above our bed.

I managed to get her towards the lifts, but she was looking at the roulette tables like a starving woman.

'Oh, come on, Rodney, we're only here for one night.'

'Oh, but I think we should . . .?'

But she'd already had a silver dollar down on red twenty-two. It won!

The croupier looked at her. 'Madam, da minimum stake is two silver dollars, but lady ah'm going to pay yer.'

So she put her two silver dollars on red twenty-two again and it won – a second time! Daphne screamed as the chips were shovelled towards her.

I panicked. 'For God's sake, Daphne, cash 'em in now, enough's enough. Don't play any more!'

Reluctantly she scooped up all those lovely chips and turned away from the table.

We got undressed in our purple and gold suite. At last we climbed into bed and I am tired . . . but not that tired. We both looked up into the mirror at the same moment, and Daphne said, 'Oh . . . we look awful!'

(*Left*) With Albert, the cat

(*Above*) In *Dear Mother, Love Albert* with
Christine Hargreaves and John Scott Martin
(*Below*) My mother and father visit the set of
Dear Mother, Love Albert + Auntie Elsie + Edna
with two Uncle Jims!

FACING PAGE
Bob and Terry at the pub…
then back at Bob's

(*Left*) With Thelma (Brigid Forsyth)

(*Above*) Me, Terry, Thelma with Noel Dyson as Thelma's mum and Anita Carey as Terry's girlfriend (Thelma's sister).

(*Below*) Bob and Thelma's wedding with Bill Owen as Thelma's dad.

With Daphne on
my wedding day
(*Inset*) With Tom Courtenay
and Ian La Frenais

My favourite picture of Daphne

On the beach at Cornwall

(*Above*) *This is Your Life* with Dick Clement and flanked by the Beastly fisherman, Burgess Nigel, Mad Monk, Pedro and Plugger!

(*Above*) With the triplets, Daphne and Daisy

(*Right*) With Daisy

(*Above*) My pantomime dame

(*Left*) Relaxing at home
in Henley-on-Thames

(*Above*) In my one man show,
Three Men in a Boat
(Photo credit: John Clarke)

(*Right*) As Mr Pooter
in *Diary of a Nobody*
(Photo credit: John Clarke)

Chapter 22

I HAD A LOVELY time in bonny Glasgow, being Noah in a play for television. In the street – was it Sauchiehall Street? – a guy grabbed the lapels of my jacket and thrust his face into mine. I caught a whiff of the Highlands and it wasn't the heather.

'Don't think I don't know who you are!'

So typical Glasgow. I'm walking along minding my own business, not a thought in my head . . .

'Don't think I don't know . . .' he was saying, 'don't assume, mate I'm a low-brow peasant that hasn't been to university, just because I'm swaying here in the gutters of Sauchiehall Street. I know who you are! OK?'

Once, some years later, at Castle Urquart on Loch Ness a Highlander looked closely at me and said, 'It's yourself isn't it?'

'Aye.'

And that's the difference between Glasgow and the Highlands, you see.

Back in London after our three happy weeks in Glasgow, Michael Cameron fixed for Daphne to have a scan. I took her to the hospital but got bored with waiting. 'Look, I don't need to be here, you could get a bus home. You don't really . . .'

'Oh, go.'

Driving over Vauxhall Bridge in the silver Bentley, I suddenly thought, 'Rodney, what are you doing?' and I went back.

I saw Daphne at the end of a long corridor in one of those cotton shifts that tie up at the back, coming through double doors. I called, 'What did they say?' She was a long way down the corridor. Heads turned to look as she slowly raised an arm and gave me a two-fingered salute, and it wasn't with the palm facing me, the one Churchill made famous, that means victory – oh, no. This two-fingered salute, going up and down meant TWINS!

Daphne was livid. 'Twins, I'm having twins! What happens now?'

'Come on, I'm taking you out to lunch.'

We went to Meridiana, upstairs, on the Fulham Road. It was a long lunch.

'I think it's wonderful, er . . . a miracle,' I said.

'Are you completely . . . how are we to cope? I had a career.'

There was another phone call from the boss of EMI Films.

'What about The Ivy?'

He didn't know I had been to LA, didn't know I was off back there, this time to return with a script. 'Oh, Mr Cohen, I'm just off on a trip and then we must meet. Only a couple of weeks.'

On one of those typical Hollywood nights, I was having dinner at Chasens in Beverly Hills with Alan Ladd Jnr, the head of production of 20th-Century Fox. Laddie had asked me to a family celebration of his daughter Kellie's birthday and we had a cake with sixteen candles on it.

I looked up and there, across the room, was Nat Cohen. He was with two tall ladies, like the ones I had seen on stage at the MGM Grand.

Had he seen me? Was he thinking, 'What's that Lively Boy doing with the boss of Fox? Is that why he won't have lunch with me?' Now he stood up, leaving the showgirls, and came over. He greeted Laddie and he was talking blah, blah, blah, EMI, and Laddie's talking blah, blah, blah Fox, and then, always polite: 'My daughters, Kellie and Tracy, my wife Pattie you've met and do you know Rodney?'

Mr Cohen turned to me. 'Rodney! At last we meet!'

'Mr Cohen, we now have a script, er . . . we have something to talk about.'

He put a friendly hand on my shoulder. 'Rodney, call me Nat!'

Jimmy Bolam's agent was asking for first billing on *The Likely Lads* film. He didn't know, and never would know, how much I had done to get the film off the ground, fixed the director and first assistant and been to Hollywood to get the screenplay together. We had always alternated the billing on the TV series, one week me and then Jim. So it was always fair.

I told my agent, Peter Crouch, 'See if he'll come into the office and we'll toss a coin.' Peter laughed but Jimmy came, and I told him my idea about tossing a coin. We tossed a coin and he won (thank goodness).

But when the poster was finalised I was given something called 'stepped billing', nothing to do with me, it just happened that way.

Emotion Blazes	Nat Cohen presents an EMI film
Across the Big Screen	
As Bob and Terry Knock	RODNEY BEWES
Down the Frontiers	
Of Human Knowledge and	[JAMES BOLAM]
Newcastle Ale	

The
LIKELY LADS   A.Cert
co-starring BRIGIT FORSYTH

Because my name was up higher, it stood out far more than so-called 'First Billing'.

One day, during filming, all I had to do all day was cross the road, a busy shopping street. Kip, our first assistant director, needed to find somewhere for me to sit between takes, and asked: 'Rod, do you mind sitting in Timpson's shoe shop? There are two very pretty ladies in there. Only this is going to take some time to set up each take.'

'How pretty, Kip?'

'Very.'

'I don't mind.'

And I didn't. They were lovely, and . . . 'Ee you're just like your face.'

'Aye, come in pet, mek yourself at 'ome like.'

Soon a lorry arrived with a huge delivery of shoes in big cardboard boxes. I took off my overcoat and jacket, undid my waistcoat and fell to help the two girls hump boxes to the store-room at the back of the shop.

We were sitting in the store-room, recovering, when the shop doorbell announced tinkle, tinkle, a customer. We looked into the shop – there was a little old lady. I begged the girls, 'Can I serve her, oh, go on, please?'

'Aye, why not, pet?'

I walked into the shop doing up my waistcoat. 'Can I help you, madam?'

She stared, mouth open . . . then . . . 'Ee, it's you, isn't it? Bob, from the . . . but what ar' ya doin' in here?'

'I work here.'

'Gerrayway, ya down't.'

'AH DO! The television's not regular, you know. That's only three months of the year and I've got mouths to feed, like. There's another nine mouths with nothing coming in. I've got to do something.'

'Ee, well pet, but ah'm in here often!'

'Now what is it I can, ere . . . is there something?'

'Aye, there is Bob, the slippers in the window, the ones wi' the red pompom.'

'For yourself, madam?'

'That's right, for me, size six.'

'If you'd care to sit down. Er, take a seat?'

One of the girls was already holding the box out ready.

'Here we are, the ones with the red pompom. Size six.'

'Ee, that was quick.'

'Oh aye, I knew just where to put me hands on 'em, ha!' I opened up the box and produced the slipper as if we were doing Cinderella. I helped her off with her fur-lined bootee. 'It fits, it fits!'

Muffled noises from the girls in the store-room.

I'm on location in glorious Newcastle and Whitley Bay, pretending to be someone else. Or am I? How much of Bob Ferris is me now and vice versa? I've spent so much time with Ian since we began in 1964. I've been Bob for over ten years, well, off and on, while he's been getting more like me.

We spent Christmas in Cornwall, then back to London for the New Year. Daphne had her bags packed and we were in the same room at the same posh private clinic with champagne and Guinness and smoked salmon and rye bread ready. She was sitting up watching colour television with an epidural drip in her back and a cannula in the back of her hand.

I'm in a far worse state than I was when Daisy Dot was born – and I was dreadful then. I can only pace. I can't believe it's twins.

'Have something to eat, Rodney.' It's the way she says 'Rodney' like that.

'I can't, I can't, I can't.'

Nurses were fussing around as was the anaesthetist. I knew she was in the best hands, Michael Cameron is a star act. I wandered the corridor, then suddenly Michael appeared, splendid in his all-green outfit, them mask round his neck.

'Rodney, I'd like to ask you to sit down.'

'What? I don't wanna sit down, I'm . . .'

'I insist you sit down.'

'Oh come off it, Michael, people only say that in films. "I insist you sit down" . . . in real life . . . you don't . . .'

'Sit DOWN!'

I sat.

'Rodney, Daphne hasn't had two, she's had three babies, all boys and they are all fine. Now, I know what you feel about the delivery room, but I want you to come with me now. Daphne is in a state of er . . . anger!'

I didn't think I could get up.

'I have given her an injection and in a few minutes she will sleep. You must come now.'

I was aware of going into the delivery room, and that I was doing a funny walk, like Alec Guinness, striding, arms swinging, in an exaggerated way. All around me bustle, the nurses busy, busy, washing, scrubbing, wiping stainless steel, water running, but I could only focus on Daphne and the way she was looking at me. She didn't look sleepy, if anything, she looked accusing, indicting. 'Well done!' I said, rather loudly. 'What a blessing!'

Oh, I know, in the novel or the screenplay you would hone it and phrase it better, but in real life you come out with something like that.

When she was sleeping I left her and went looking for our handsome gynaecologist. I found him staring out of a window.

'Look, Rodney, I'd like you to see this.' I looked out into the car park at the front of the building. 'I had those two ambulances standing by to take the babies in incubators to University College Hospital into intensive care, just in case. I've just rung down to send them away.'

He's telling me something, I thought. He means they're all OK. I couldn't speak and my eyes were so hot. Damn.

'Would you like to go and see the boys?'

'Oh . . . yeah . . . please.'

'In there.'

I went in. Five or six Perspex oblong boxes, three of them occupied.

The sister spoke in a soft Irish accent. 'Now, father, would you like t'feed one?'

'Oh, could I? Yes, please.'

They sat me down and showed me how to hold the bottle of clear sweetened liquid. It was one of the greatest moments of my life, ever.

Three little faces, still red and blotchy, and those tiny hands, resting in their own see-through Perspex worlds. I read the labels.

BEWES I   5lbs 2oz

BEWES II   3lbs 11oz

BEWES III   3lbs 6oz

My boys! Joe, Tom, and Bill! I drove to Jimmy Bolam's house where he and Sue were sweet to me. Jimmy gave me a big glass of red wine, but I found I could only sip it. I felt I didn't need it. I had another high, far stronger than alcohol.

Sue asked after Daphne. Jimmy made a gesture with his thumb flicking in and out of his fist. 'Oh, Daphne'll be OK . . . like shelling peas!'

I rang everyone. I rang Ian in Hollywood and told him to tell Dick and Laddie and Pattie.

'Er, Rodney?' said Ian, 'what was that story about Daphne in Bombay with Barbara Hulanicki? They went to a temple and Barbara said not to touch the great stone symbol erect in the centre of the floor. But Daf did touch it and oh, poor Daf! So you see, Rodney, it wasn't anything to do with you!'

Jimmy Bolam told me a story over lunch. We had done the last shot of the Likely Lads movie and had repaired to the big Trusthouse Forte hotel near the airport. We ordered a nice bottle of wine, and Jim looked very thoughtful. Then out it came: 'I'm driving along from our house towards the Fulham Palace Road and Susan says, "James?" Yes, I says. "Er, you know Daphne's had three, well I'm just having the one!" I nearly crashed the car. I went up on the pavement, nearly hit a lamppost, then bump, bump back on to the road!'

We laughed and laughed. What a wonderful way of breaking the news, I thought.

Chapter 23

THE GRAND OPENING of our *Likely Lads* film was in Newcastle upon Tyne.

I saw Jimmy Bolam arrive. The journalists asked the inevitable – 'I bet it's great to be back?'

'Look, I took the last train in and I shall catch the first train out.'

Oh, I think I know what he meant, but it was not what they wanted to hear. I think you are supposed to be thrilled to be back, aren't you?

The next day all the papers carried the quote 'Likely Lad shuns homeland!'

Tom Courtenay rang. 'Cheryl's left home.'

'I'm coming round.'

I took a fine claret, gently cradled in my arms, let myself in and climbed to the first floor sitting-room to find Tom practising putting. At the end of the carpet was a metal thingy you can tap the balls into. He was standing with his club, digging it into the deep pile of the carpet.

'Y'see Rodney, it's, er, all t'do with the, er, grip . . . no, your grip is er . . . y'see, this hand above like, the er thumb so . . . this hand like so . . . the thumb leading down the er . . . no, grip, it's all about your grip.'

He didn't talk about Cheryl, he talked about golf. I sat on the big sofa listening dutifully until I became so bored I picked up my bottle of claret and went home. I put it back in the cellar and poured myself a Berry Bros good, ordinary claret instead.

A few days later, the telephone rang again.

'Oh, er, hello, Rodney? Only I would like to er . . . come round. Need to, er . . .?'

'Fine, fine . . . sure, sure . . . see you in a sec.'

I was sitting on the sofa again, Tom across the room, standing, preparing. Again I wasn't expected to say anything, just listen. Tom cleared his throat.

'No, . . . er, y'see, Rodney' (he always says my name as if there's something he doesn't quite understand, something inexplicable in the air) '. . . no, I er . . . Cheryl and I. Are, er, basically . . . two, er . . . this isn't easy . . . no.'

Cheryl had moved back into their home with daughter Sam, and Tom moved in with me.

Late at night, Daf and I were watching a Swedish film on television. Liv Ullmann turned to her lover and said in his ear, 'Ule dule femton uhhra doffe coffa nahhna?'

The subtitles read: 'Take me, take me, take me.'

I said to Daf, 'You never say that to me.'

We went to bed and just as I was dropping off, she started whispering in my ear, 'Take me, take me, TAKE ME!'

'Daphne, for God's sake, I was just dropping off. What's the matter with you? Honestly! Frightened me to death.'

'Goodnight, love.'

'Night.'

Later, we both woke at the same moment. What the . . .? Someone was trying to break the front door down.

Tom popped his head into our bedroom. 'Only, er . . . it'll be for me . . . I think, er . . . don't get up.'

We heard him go downstairs and open the front door. Daphne gave me a raised eyebrow 'what's up now?' look. I shrugged 'who knows?' then we heard sounds of a scuffle, what sounded to me like Bunter being set upon by the fourth remove.

'OW, OW, OW Stop . . . Owow ow, don't . . . ow, ow, ow, oh!'

Then a lady's voice. 'Goodnight!'

Door slams shut.

Then Tom's coming back upstairs, he comes back into our bedroom. Now he's limping.

'Only me . . . er, that was Cheryl . . . she's gone now. Er, night, night.'

'Oh, shall I make some tea, or owt?'

'No, no, see you in the morning, night Daphne.'

'Goodnight, Tom.'

Scene 18A: EXT. CLIFFTOPS DAY

(A WIDE PANORAMIC VIEW OF THE MOUTH OF THE TYNE, SHOWING THE TWIN PIERS, THE CURVE OF THE RIVER, AND DOCKYARDS AND THE SEA BEYOND. CAMERA ZOOMS IN SLOWLY ON TO NORTH PIER, ON WHICH A FEW FIGURES ARE FISHING. THEY ARE IN WELLINGTONS AND ANORAKS PROTECTING THEM AGAINST THE COLD NORTHERN SUNDAY MORNING.)

(THAT WAS WRITTEN IN SOUTHERN CALIFORNIA,
IT WAS BLOODY FREEZING.)

Scene 18B: ANOTHER ANGLE

(SHOWS THAT Terry IS ONE OF THE ANGLERS. WITH
A CIGARETTE IN HIS MOUTH HE EXPERTLY BAITS
AND CASTS HIS LINE. HE IS A CONTENTED MAN.
BESIDE HIM HE HAS A THERMOS, A *NEWS OF THE
WORLD* AND A SIX-PACK OF MCEWANS EXPORT.)

Scene 18C: CAR PARK DAY

(THERE IS A CAR PARK BESIDE A COVE AT THE BASE
OF THE PIER; SEVERAL SMALL FISHING BOATS ARE
BEACHED THERE. Bob's CAR PULLS INTO THE
PARKING AREA.)

Scene 18D: EXTERIOR PIER DAY

(CLOSE ON Terry. HE HAS HIS ROD WEDGED AND IS
READING THE PAPER. ANOTHER ANGLE AS Bob
APPROACHES HIM. HE IS CASUALLY, THOUGH
SMARTLY, DRESSED FOR SUNDAY MORNING.)

BOB: Terry!

(Terry LOOKS ROUND WITH PLEASANT SURPRISE.)

TERRY: Hello, kidda . . . I thought you played badminton
            Sundays.

BOB: Not this week. Thelma has bruised toes.

TERRY: Oh dear.

BOB: I dropped a brick.

TERRY: You're always dropping bricks, Bob.

BOB: This one was on her foot in the library.

(Bob GAZES OUT TO SEA, REFLECTIVELY, SHAKING HIS HEAD AT THE BITTER MEMORY.)

TERRY: D'you want some coffee? I'd offer you a beer but I've only got six cans.

BOB: No thanks.

(THERE IS A PAUSE.)

TERRY: I had some news this week . . . me divorce came through.

BOB: Really?

TERRY: Aye, I was going to give you a call and go out for a few jars, but then I thought if we celebrate my divorce it might give Thelma grounds for yours.

BOB: What were your grounds in the end?

TERRY: Just about everything except insanity. Although I must have been insane to get married in the first place.

BOB: How d'you feel about it?

TERRY: Same as I felt about the Fat Ox coming down. There goes yesterday.

BOB: (THE PESSIMIST) The street coming down really upset me. Because it reminded me how much of our past is gone.

(PAUSE.)

BOB: (CONT.) Oh, it's different for you. With your divorce and your new job and your flat. Your changes are happening now. My future's all bogged down.

TERRY: (LOOKS AT HIM, NOT WITHOUT SYMPATHY) Oh, go on, you can have a beer if you want one.

BOB: (TAKES A CAN AND POPS IT OPEN, THEN LOOKS OUT TO SEA AND SAYS, REFLECTIVELY) In the chocolate box of life, the top layer's already gone. And someone's pinched the coffee cream from the bottom . . .

TERRY: (looking at him, eyes widening) Bloody hell . . .

I was very fond of a speech that Bob made playing bridge in a caravan with Terry and Thelma and Terry's girlfriend Chris.

BOB: I always had this fear of being on a slow boat to somewhere. One of those tramp steamers in the Indian Ocean. There's Ava Gardner, Wilfrid Hyde-White, me and a man in dark glasses with one arm who got on at Tangier. Four strangers thrown together by a whim of fate – and I was the only one who couldn't play bridge. I'd be an outcast. I'd spend the nights pacing the poop deck. Their jollity and laughter taunting me through the porthole. And by the time we got to Madagascar, Ava would belong to the one-armed man.

TERRY:	How did he shuffle?
BOB:	Pardon?
TERRY:	How did he shuffle with one arm?
BOB:	Well, I don't know, do I, not being in the cabin with the others.

I wondered if the film would make my fortune. I had a percentage, five per cent after costs, and the film certainly didn't cost a lot. Less than £300,000. Albert Finney had been around the world and became a millionaire from his percentage of Tony Richardson's *Tom Jones*. Would *The Likely Lads* film set me up for life? I don't think so, and writing this, twenty-nine years on, I haven't received a penny, nothing, nought, zilch . . . Jimmy Bolam, at the same time we tossed that coin for billing on the posters, declined a percentage, saying, 'No, thank you, who wants five per cent of f★★★ all!'

Perhaps he knew something I didn't?

Now with all the publicity for the film behind me, it was time to join my family in Cornwall. So nice to be back in the village, get the Sunday papers and oh, dear, an article about me, and there's a story about . . . I must ring Jimmy Bolam.

'Jimmy? There's a piece in the paper . . . now don't get angry . . . well, it's about the film and the Likely Lads . . . but she tells that story about Sue in the car, you know, "Daphne's had three, well I'm just having the one!" I can't believe I told that story to a . . . are you there?'

Stony silence at the other end, then, 'Did you? Did you tell a story about my private life to . . .?'

He was furious. I could hear it in the silence.

'Jim, look I had to do so many interviews – you don't do them. Yes, I might have done. I didn't know it was a secret. I've heard that story told in Gerry's Club. I've heard Peter Crouch tell it . . . look, I didn't know it wasn't in public domain, you know fine well . . . I swear to God I don't think I told her! The story's been knocking around for, er, nearly five months.'

'You, you're willing to swear in a lawyer's office, you didn't?'

'Well, no, Jimmy . . . look . . .'

He put the phone down, oh damn, damn, damn. Oh, I wished, I wished I could undo that . . .

Was it that bad? It was to someone like Bolam. I rang him back but he didn't answer the phone and I never spoke to him again. He never spoke to me again. It's been nearly thirty years. We have never met, never bumped into each other in the theatre or voice-over studio in Soho. I've always thought how funny it would be to see him walking down a corridor towards me at the Television Centre or at Granada or Yorkshire Television . . . but it hasn't happened . . . yet.

There were lots of things we were asked to do as *The Likely Lads*: the Royal Variety Show, commercials, plays and lucrative summer seasons at the seaside, but that wasn't to be. He refused to come on my *This Is Your Life* in 1980, and Thames Television even had to find a clip that didn't include my co-star!

Once, while being interviewed to publicise a stage play I was touring in, the journalist told me he had interviewed Jimmy in the same theatre dressing-room a couple of years earlier. The publicist of Jimmy's play had told him he could only interview Jimmy if he made no mention of *The Likely Lads*! The journalist told me, 'It was very hard on me because I'm the biggest fan of the programme!'

The worst thing is I've lied about it ever since. I've toured lots of plays, and recently, the one-man show I do. Every week I have to talk to the local papers, radio stations, magazines and appear on TV shows, and it's always the same question: 'And your mate? Do you still see him?'

'Oh yeah, sure, sure, we're great friends . . . usually meet up for a meal, least once a week – oh, certainly.'

It's not true but it stops all further discussion and it's what most people want to hear. It is just so much easier than saying, 'No, we haven't seen each other, or spoken to each other since *The Likely Lads* film came out, and that was in 1976!'

I often think about what David Robinson said in *The Times*, 15th April 1976: '*The Likely Lads* is one of television's happiest creations . . .'

Chapter 24

I HAD AN INTERVIEW with a Hollywood director for a film. They asked me what time would suit me. I told them the end of the day. I had been up with the boys the night before. Things were pretty fraught at home. Both Daisy and Daphne had chickenpox.

I presented myself at the Wellington Suite at the Inn On The Park to meet Peter Bogdanovich. It was getting late and I was too comfortable, too warm in a wing armchair. Bogdanovich asked me if I wanted a drink and I heard myself asking for a vodka and tonic. He gave me a very large one.

Then he was pacing up and down, being a movie director. 'The scene is exterior Singapore Docks night.'

You know that feeling when you think you are going to fall asleep although you don't want to? Watching TV or at the theatre? Your eyes begin to close and your head nods . . .

The scene is exterior Singapore Docks night.'

My head touched the top of my chest and I was asleep.

'Rodney, Rodney!' He was shaking me. He was livid. All I could think about was thank goodness I had put my glass down. 'I've seen four hundred goddam English actors this week and you are the first one that's fallen asleep on me, for chrissake!'

'Yes, but you'll remember me, won't you?'

Cheeky – but I got the part!

I was flattered by a piece in the *Evening Standard*, Friday 31st March 1978:

THE ARTS Sydney Edwards.

UNLIKELY LAD

[Sydney Edwards was that rare showbiz journalist, one that everybody liked and respected.]

Mr Bewes is of some social significance in the theatre and TV, although he would be surprised to hear you say so. He was very much in the middle of that new wave of English realism in the Sixties, at the time of *Saturday Night and Sunday Morning*, *A Kind of Loving*, *Z-Cars*.

I'm to meet James Villiers at the airport, but there is no sign. Then at last there he is, tall in a perfect 'country' overcoat and topped out with a straw boater with Leander ribbon. Every inch the aristocrat.

'Thought you were gonna miss it, Jim.'

'Came out to the airport with some chums, had a few large ones!'

'What's with the boater?'

'It's Leander, lovey.'

'You rowed for Leander?'

'No, I drank for them!'

He had a few more large ones on the plane. When we arrived in the Far East and met up in Peter Bogdanovich's suite at the hotel that night with Ben Gazzara and Denholm Elliott, he greeted our illustrious director, still wearing the boater, with 'AH, Bogdanovich,

Pedro. I do hope this one is going to be better than your last. You need a hit, lovey!'

And to Ben Gazzara, the star of our film, 'Benjy Baby, get me a Jimbo, will you? A large gin, lime, a ton of ice and a splash of soda. Have you got that?'

And the Americans adored him.

At the endless rehearsals Peter Bogdanovich changed everything, and Ben Gazzara repeated everything he said.

'Oh, let's rewrite this scene, it's no good!'

'Yeah, let's rewrite this scene, it's no good.'

Peter Bogdanovich hired a huge white Daimler and sat in the back being driven about while smoking a very long Havana cigar. Gazzara seemed content to smoke the Montecristo number three I'd bought duty-free at Heathrow. He kept saying he would replace them but never did.

We filmed from five in the evening until five the next morning. One day, as we came out of the hotel to go to work there was the long white Daimler with Peter Bogdanovich in the back. He pressed the window button and swish, down went the window. 'Oh Denholm! I've changed the schedule, I shall start with 467, all right?'

'Sure, chief, lovely.'

And swish, up went the window so the air conditioning could get to work, and off he went gliding down the curved drive and on to Paterson Road, leaving Denholm and me to walk in the heat and dust. Sure, the location was only two or three blocks down Orchard Road, but . . .

I told Denholm about making *The Three Musketeers* with Charlton Heston, Michael York and Oliver Reed. One lunchtime, Raquel Welch, very glamorous and bursting out of a white towelling bathrobe asked me what I'd been doing lately.

'Oh, er, crabbing . . . in the cove.'

'Er . . . crabbing?'

I don't think she knew what I meant. 'Yeah, with Plugger and Pedro . . . oh, and the Mad Monk.'

'Oh? Fun?'

As soon as I was back in Cornwall, propping up the bar, everyone had the same question.

What was Raquel Welch really like . . . really?

'Oh, you know, she was such a drag. A pain, really. "Oh, Rodney, I only want to come in for a coffee". Yeah, sure, I thought, *and* the rest. "Rodney, I only want to sit on your bed and talk."'

'She never . . . no?'

'Naw, course she never!'

'Bewesey, you're such a bloody liar!'

'I had lunch with her though. Really.'

'What did she have on? When you had the er . . . lunch with her, like, what was she wearing?'

'S'more what she didn't have on, mate. She had on this white towelling bathrobe, and nothing underneath!'

'BEWESEY!!'

'Take him outside and scrag him.'

'Take him outside and hose him down.'

Tatty Muirhead started up a verse of 'What shall we do with a drunken sailor?' with the words 'What shall we do about Bewesey's stories?'

And it was my round.

That winter we were snowed in, a most unheard of thing, in Cornwall. No one could get up the two steep hills outside the village.

The power lines were down and at night the village looked like a Christmas card, with candles flickering at cottage windows.

Our neighbours in London rang with some disturbing news, saying they could hear running water in our new house on Barnes Common.

'You have a key, do go and see, and ring us back.'

We waited, anxiously, for five minutes, ten minutes . . . they seemed to be an awfully long time, then, 'Hello Rodney, we've been in your house . . . wearing wellies.' WEARING WELLIES?

A pipe had burst in the attic and water had poured through ceilings, over pictures and books, bringing down cornices. In despair I rang my best friend Tom, who lived not far away. I asked him what we should do and he gave us some advice, a great balm to Daphne and me in our time of need and ever since.

'Well Rodney, I think you should dig deep into your humanity.'

Thanks, Tom.

On 16th June, I opened in *Middle-Aged Spread* at the Lyric Theatre. I was thrilled Lucy Fleming was in it, and terrified that Celia Johnson, her clever and funny mother, would come and see us.

Tom was at the Queen's Theatre in Ronald Harwood's *The Dresser*, so we could go home together on the bus.

Middle-Aged Spread by Roger Hall won the Comedy of the Year Award. The producer, Bill Kenwright, told me he wanted to pop in and see us one day, but couldn't, as we were full up.

Tom's character, theatrical dresser in the play of the same name, is, as they say, a great creation. More prissy than camp in Fair Isle pullover with pins and needles and safety pins always at the ready. Freddie Jones was wonderful as the theatrical knight whom Norman dresses, so vulnerable you think this evening's play might be the last for him.

Down the road at the Lyric, I was scared of *my* dresser, Cliff, who said things like, 'My, oh my, we are late getting ready tonight, aren't we?' and 'Don't we look peaky tonight, hmm? Too many late nights!' And when I said, 'S'going well tonight!' for want of anything *to* say, he said, 'Oh, do you think so? I've been out front!'

Chapter 25

WE HAD A LOVELY long summer 'on the Avenue' as theatre folk say. Lucy Fleming, my leading lady, was separated from her husband Joe, and friends with Simon Williams, who was also in the West End.

One terrible Sunday evening in December, dark clouds and gales and very cold, I was told of a tragedy on the river. Joe and his daughter Flora, aged nine, had both drowned at Battersea Reach.

There had been a party on Joe's boat, moored off the Chelsea Embankment. Joe and Flora were going ashore in a tiny inflatable dinghy when a third man tried to get into the dinghy. It capsized and, though they were wearing life jackets, they never reached the steps on the river wall.

The river police told me it was one of the worst nights they had ever seen on the river; high tide and high winds. They told me too it could take three weeks for bodies to come up from the river, and they might get snagged on pilings, sunken timbers or jetties and the like.

I knew Lucy would be thinking of coming back to the play, but I also knew she mustn't. I had to do the play without Lucy. I wanted to go and see her. I wanted to drive down to Nettlebed near Henley where Lucy lived with her two boys, but I had to do the play.

Two weeks later, on 1st January, there was still no news from the river police, who never stopped searching, and Lucy insisted coming back to the play. I thought it was too soon, but couldn't say so.

She was fine in the play that first night back, except her shoulders shook right up until the end of the play, as if she couldn't control them. Everything else she could control, but not her shoulders.

In *Middle-Aged Spread*, we are having an affair, Lucy's character and mine, so we faced each other, looked into each other's eyes, held each other. It was very hard for Lucy because we knew each other's families, there was too much real life between us.

At the matinee on Wednesday, Lucy nearly went, her eyes first of all glazed over and her shoulders began to shake again violently, and I held her on stage and the two of us shared the moment. No one else knew.

On Sunday, the river police rang to say they had found the body of the other man in the dinghy, near the spot where the accident happened at Battersea Reach. Exactly three weeks, just as the river police had said it would be. Then they rang the next day to say they had found 'the little girl'. Then I heard a catch in the voice. 'By Westminster Bridge . . . she didn't look too bad . . . she had one of those digital watches, it was still flashing up red numbers . . . on her little wrist.'

At the theatre I went round all the dressing-rooms telling the cast. No one asked if Lucy would be coming back. I told the understudy she must take over Lucy's room. I packed up her things.

On Wednesday I went to the big Victorian church at Roehampton. When I got home the telephone was ringing. They had found Joe's body at Hammersmith. I was so glad it was nearly over, for Lucy's sake.

★

Tom's play came off on the 17th January, and we were to finish on February 7th. I had some very good nights in the play. When I had lots of energy and really went for it, I terrified the others.

Tom's last night, we all went to Chez Victor. I sat near the window of the restaurant and I could see up the street to the side of the Queen's, Tom's set coming out and being loaded on to the huge van.

At the Savoy, at the *Evening Standard* Awards Lunch, Tom was Actor of the Year. He made a very good speech and so did Sir Ralph Richardson who was still calling me 'Starry'.

On my last night in *Middle-Aged Spread*, the 'House Full' boards were still outside. I overheard one of the actresses say as she came down the dressing-room stairs, 'Oh if only I can drag myself through it tonight.'

This was before the play had started, at a time when I'm always rubbing hands together like a football fan before the game.

Dark clouds and a terrible night. In south-west Cornwall, the Penlee Lifeboat was lost with all hands. Eight crewmen left five widows and eight orphans.

Our Lizard lifeboat searched all night and all the next day, finding pieces of the wreckage, bits of double diagonal ply, painted a very dark blue and highly polished, an oilskin coat and a bobble hat.

Pedro, Burgess, Leggey, Peter Pan and Old Man were looking for mates, people they knew.

Chapter 26

AFTER THE BOYS' first day at school, I was dying to know what they thought of it. They came tumbling into the house all socks and bags, saying, 'We've met Edward Cole!'

It was the only topic.

'He sits next to Tom!'

I wondered why Edward was so special.

'He told us in the playground.'

'Yes?'

'He's been in outer space!'

'I see.'

I did a BBC television play: Sheridan's *The Critic* was good for my morale which was very low, as was the bank balance. *The Critic* was in the BBC's Play of the Month series with a cast and sets to make it Play of the Year, including Rosemary Leach, Nigel Hawthorne, Alan Badel, Anna Massey, John Gielgud and Matthew Kelly.

After rehearsals when we finally moved into the studio at the Television Centre to film, the settings, the staging and colours were fabulous, like an Inigo Jones masque. One evening after a supper break we were heading back to the studio, along the curved corridor on the dressing-room floor, when coming towards us around the bend was Rod Steiger. The others went silent, recognising the star of *On the Waterfront* and *In the Heat of the Night*. I said, 'Oh Rod, I popped into your rehearsal. Just one thing, don't look at the lens, destroys the illusion, love.'

'Oh no, did I?' said Rod, 'I'm so used to a big movie camera!'

When I got back to our studio, Anna Massey asked me, 'And how, pray, do you know Rod Steiger?'

'Oh, he comes to a class I run in Seven Dials, you know, near the Cambridge Theatre.'

And they all jumped on me.

'Hey, mind the costume! Honestly, some people . . .'

A letter to treasure:

Dear Mr Bewes,
I have pleasure in advising you that at the ballot held on April 1st, you were elected a full member of the Garrick Club.

Daphne said it was the first step to becoming an old fogey, but she was just trying to spoil it for me. I was very pleased, not least because of my background. I'd love to have been able to take my father, with his mac over one shoulder and his cycle clips.

At the end of April, Celia Johnson died. I heard she'd been at home near Henley after a week of previews of a new play, and opening-night looming. It was Sunday afternoon and she was playing bridge with friends.

'Now, just wait a minute . . .' she said. A couple of seconds later she was unconscious.

Peter Fleming, the colonel, had died quite suddenly after loosing off two barrels of his shotgun in Scotland, and now Celia, while finessing the Queen of Diamonds.

I shall always remember her telling me off because I had pointed out that she had licked her lips whilst describing how handsome Gerald du Maurier was.

In the *Daily Express*, Jean Rook wrote:

'We can get back the Falklands. We can never replace Celia Johnson.'

Lionel Blair was in my kitchen – a surprise visitor – and it was not yet nine o'clock in the morning! He was planning a pantomime. He was saying 'Give me a Goldilocks that is blonde and sixteen and can sing and dance and act in front of five hundred PEOPLE!'

When he said 'people' he flung his arms out like a ringmaster announcing the trapeze artistes.

'Lionel, don't do that, I haven't had a cup of coffee yet.'

'Do *you* do Panto? Next year . . . come to Richmond for me. You could be a beautiful ugly SISTER! Anna Neagle's going to be the Fairy QUEEN!'

'Lionel!'

'I want YOU! And if you want to do it, start wearing high heels, NOW! Bye, love to Daf.'

Where would I get a pair of high heels from? Not in Daphne's wardrobe.

So I borrowed a pair of high heels from Beverly Jones, who stroked the ladies' Eight at the Moscow Olympics, and wore them around the house.

Angela Cole brought Joe, Tom, and Bill home from tea with

Edward. I tottered along the hall in those high heels to open the front door.

'Oh, they were ever so good . . .' She was looking at those heels.

'Thanks so much for bringing them home.' I wonder, should I say anything? No . . . leave it. She'll go home and tell her husband. 'Funny thing, you know Daphne's Rodney? He wears high heels around the house.'

At rehearsals, Lionel despaired at ever teaching me even a few dance steps. Thank goodness for long skirts, I thought. We rehearsed near Twickenham. Morecambe and Wise were in the next room. Eric stuck his head around the door as Lionel was pulling out his hair.

'Rubbish!'

'It is, love . . . I've got an Ugly Sister with two left feet!'

'Ugly Sister? He's far too pretty. Swap parts with him Lionel . . . all right Rodders?'

My friend, Eric Morecambe.

Kenneth Connor, who had been in twenty *Carry On* films, was called Sue Ellen, and I'm Raquel . . .

On the first night at the beautiful Richmond Theatre on the Green: 'Raquel, love, you come on to your music [the theme from *Dallas*] and you walk straight down to the floats [footlights] and you do this [that gesture he did in my kitchen], then you wait.'

'Lionel, I can't.'

'You do it! The band play your music and you go down to the floats and wait for your round!'

The band were playing the overture and Lionel spotted a card, the back of a playbill on a nail. On it the stage hand had written the order of the scenes. Lionel took it down and there really were tears in his eyes. 'Oh look everyone! Scene One, FAIRYLAND!!'

When it was time for my first entrance, I heard my music and on I went down to the floats. I flung my arms in the air and there was a terrific round of applause. I turned to where I knew Lionel was watching in the wings and gave him a most enormous wink. He was blowing kisses.

I took the make-up very seriously, I found out about a place near Eton Square where models go to try make-up. Cosmetics à la carte was very grand, a row of American-style barber's chairs and above, crystal chandeliers. I walked up and down, no shirt, a little towel on my shoulders, taking advice from girls I had only seen on the covers of *Vogue* and *Paris Match*.

'I think the eyes are too heavy, don't you?'

'The lipstick isn't YOU!'

They were all so helpful. I was having a ball.

When the Panto was on I couldn't pass a chemist's shop without popping in to try a new blusher.

I shared a dressing-room with Peter Sallis who would later become a household name in *Last of the Summer Wine*. He has a very dry humour. I would flit between the full-length mirror near him to do my mascara, then back to my own place for lip gloss or blusher. He was always trying to read *The Times*.

'Do be careful with that powder,' he said. 'I can hardly breathe! . . . How they let you into the Garrick, I don't know!'

Elaine, Sallis's wife, is sweet to me. They live in Richmond, just across the Green in a pretty terrace leading down to the river. At tea one day she told me I could stay the night any time if – after two shows and the pub – I didn't want to drive home.

'You'd be welcome to stay.'

Peter looked up from his *Times*. 'Well, not all that welcome.'

I spent a great deal of time in the wings, changing wigs and enormous costumes, then leaning with my back on the long wooden ladder to the flies. It's a journey too far to get up to the dressing-room in me frocks.

I liked to tease Anna Neagle . . . you know, one Dame to another. One night I asked her, in the dark, busy side of the stage, scenes shifting, orchestra playing, audience chattering, 'Should I stick to comedy?'

She looked at me so very seriously and whispered back, 'I don't know, Rodney, there is a depth of sadness behind your eyes, you could take tragedy in your stride.'

Oh, I thought, I must write that down before I forget it . . . Dame Anna Neagle said to me . . . Oh, if I don't write it down I'll get it wrong . . .

'There is a depth of sadness behind your eyes . . .'

Chapter 27

WE HAD A HUGE overdraft. A producer friend told me that my agent had told him over the phone 'I can't get Rodney arrested on television.' Daphne and I sat down for a big discussion. Should we sell the house in Cornwall? It would break my heart.

Spring was coming. I joined the London Rowing Club and went off in a single scull down the river towards the Houses of Parliament and up towards Richmond. I turned my back on Cornwall, arranging for the house to be let during the holidays.

Tom Courtenay's dad died the week I started rehearsals for a tour of a play called *Relative Values*. I was very sad. He was funny, walking with such a limp from an accident on Hull Fish Docks many years ago. His face would crumple into such a wicked grin and eyes twinkling. 'No, I'm just a plain working man, but . . .'

I knew the play was no good and so did the leading lady, Prunella Gee.

What had Rod Steiger told me? – 'There's only one thing worse than being in a flop, that's rehearsing a flop!'

I held a party for my mother's eightieth birthday at the Garrick Club.

The aunts and uncles came too. We had the oval table near the door in the grand Coffee Room. The long table down the centre of the room was full of members enjoying themselves, noisily.

Before I knew what was happening, Auntie Edna was up on her feet taking flash photos of our table, of Bessie Bewes, aged eighty.

How can I describe the sound that rose from the centre table? It was like that awful noise Members of Parliament make when they don't approve! Auntie Edna was squaring up to them as if to say what's the matter with you lot? The attorney general was at the end of the table, arguing with her. Then Mary, in charge of the room, shut the members up and had a quiet word in Auntie Edna's ear. Mary could have run the country. She certainly never put up with any nonsense from the members of the Garrick Club.

Peace restored, my mother said, 'Well, what a fuss. I should have liked a photo or two to remember the evening.'

'Now then, don't you worry Bessie,' said Edna. 'I've got a couple that should be beauties – if they come out!'

It was a night to remember.

Bamber Gascoigne had written a play with a Frenchman in it. I went to meet Bamber, the producer Colin Brough, and the director Mel Smith, who asked me . . . 'Do this funny French accent, we've heard so much about.'

My Frenchman is based on Alain, the restaurateur at Mon Plaisir in Monmouth Street, who says ur after every word. 'Zur ur pâté ur is ur made ur viz ur zur ur goose ur . . .'

Bamber and Colin Brough laughed, but Mel Smith said, 'Let's go and eat.'

Bamber Gascoigne's play was called *Big in Brazil*. Rehearsals were hell for me. Mel Smith vetoed everything I did. The producer had provided door frames for rehearsals instead of so many upright poles. The play was a farce so the doors were very important. Mel Smith showed me how to come through them. He showed me how to sit on a sofa, a chair, how to walk across the room. He showed me how to say a line BEFORE I had a chance to say it first, and as for that French accent, the one that got me the part . . .

'That's out! Too . . . you know? Not funny . . . now this is funny! . . . do it like that, right?'

In short he destroyed me completely. I was so unhappy and frightened and so nervous! I should have walked that first week of rehearsals – with dignity.

I never enjoyed playing the play, at Brighton, Richmond, or even the beautiful Old Vic. Even after we had been running three or four weeks, I never enjoyed it and I'm stage struck, me!

I had to do quite a few lines off, shouting through a door, that kind of thing, and I couldn't learn them. I took my script up to the wings every night and read those lines. Now at the time of writing this I do two one-man shows, both ninety minutes long, both learnt, but I never learned those lines off in *Big in Brazil*.

Daily Mail, Thursday, 20th September 1984
Big in Brazil: The Old Vic
Jack Tinker at last night's first night:

> . . . For this is quite the most graceless, witless and improbable evening any couple can expect to spend in the theatre, whichever side of the footlights they're sentenced to endure. Though the play raises a series of increasingly improbable characters, not least of whom is Mr Rodney Bewes inadequately disguised behind a very frail French accent as Feydeau, a great farceur himself.

Well, Jack, you never heard me doing Alain from *Mon Plaisir*, did you? I was only sorry for Bamber Gascoigne, who was charming about the whole thing.

A script through the door and everything changes. A television play called *The Camera Club*.

Then a money job, a training film. The training film was for a company John Cleese is a director of, Video Arts. Very highly thought of. I was sent four scripts and a nice letter from the production secretary:

> The part we would very much like you to play is that of Wally. Kenneth Williams is playing the Genie and Nerys Hughes is Joan. James Cellan Jones is the director. Our fingers and toes are tightly crossed!

Wasn't that nice? Anything was nice after working on *Big in Brazil*.

At Shepperton Studios that first morning in front of the camera, I said, 'My God, Nerys Hughes and Kenneth Williams and James Cellan Jones! I'm surrounded by the Welsh!'

Kenneth Williams said in that famous voice: 'Name one! Name one famous Welshman! You can't, can you? No . . . name one! A famous Welshman?'

'Inigo Jones!'

'Owweerr yes, he's bright, this one, isn't he the clever one!'

I think Inigo Jones was born in Smithfield in London, but there's no point in going into *that*, is there?

Some years later I was sent *The Kenneth Williams Diaries* and was interested to see what he wrote about our training film.

Monday, 4th February

To studios at Shepperton. I was used for a line-up before lunch, so I needn't have gone there till 12.30. Wardrobe and make-up girls are marvellous. I went to lunch with them. Rodney Bewes keeps up the humour and makes everybody laugh. He is very good in the role, there's no doubt of that: remarkably good, in fact. Very real.

Tuesday, 5th February

There's no let up in the pace. I get a bit annoyed at times when Bewes is doing the jokes in the middle of a sequence where I have to concentrate, and today when he did it I loudly started running my lines and drowned his conversation. He doesn't do it maliciously 'cos he's not ill-natured, he is unthinking: that's the problem.

Wednesday, 6th February

I get very tetchy during rehearsals and shooting because of the endless banter and funny sallies from Bewes and the director, and several times I said, 'Can we get on?' and stopped it . . . when one is supposed to be concentrating . . . and I find it intolerable.

I couldn't believe my eyes, because the opposite happened in reality. Kenneth Williams was the one who told jokes as if to make the crew love him. I was the one getting ratty because I had so much unlearnable dialogue.

While Daphne was away, Bernard Cribbins came to stay for a few days. We were like *The Odd Couple*. When I got back home from work, I said, 'I've got you an avocado to eat before your beans on toast, all right, love?' Then I told him I had to open a shop, a furniture store, the next morning.

'What for?'

'For money, cash. In a brown envelope, in readies, you know.'

'Cut his tie off!'

'You what?'

Bernard told me that if I had to cut a ribbon to open the store the thing to do was to cut off the managing director's/owner's tie. He assured me it always went down well.

I did it and not only was the shop owner furious, but his wife was too. 'I bought that tie for Harold for our anniversary. S'very sentimental, well, it *was!*'

Back in London, and my friend, Alan Ladd Jnr, now the boss of MGM, and Rod Steiger were in town. Rod was to get married to Paula Ellis. The reception was upstairs at Crockfords in Curzon Street. Claire Bloom was there, his wife before the one before this one, and Ronnie Harwood, on great form. Daphne looked lovely in a black trouser suit. Tom didn't come.

Rod looked sad in a blazer with a grey woollen cardigan underneath, like an old man. There was something not right. The evening broke up with Rod standing and saying, 'Well, I thank you all for coming. I'm going downstairs to gamble now.' He was to suffer from depression for quite some time after this. Tom knew, I think. I wish he'd spoken to me about it, before we went to that do.

My own star was fading like harbour lights to a night fishing boat. I knew in my heart of hearts I had to write something, as I had at the end of the Sixties, when I'd written *Dear Mother . . . Love Albert*. I started an autobiography, but it got shoved into a drawer. I called it *Tales in the Wardrobe* because, as I said before, it's a place in the theatres where the director and the producer never find you. It's a sanctuary and you can smell ironing and see girls changing their clothes, and you are given tea. I suppose any publisher would change it to *A Likely Story*.

Sunday Times, 8th January 1989

GEORDIE GREIG ON A POWER STRUGGLE OVER REPEAT SHOWINGS OF CLASSIC TV SERIES

James Bolam says 'yes' to repeat television showings of *Only When I Laugh*, but 'no' to *The Likely Lads* on video.

. . . control over which programmes are repeated lies, to a large extent, in the hands of the actors. Martin Shaw, for instance, last year refused to allow *The Professionals* to be repeated because he no longer thought it fitted his image.

This Tuesday, James Bolam, one of Britain's highest paid TV actors, will be seen on Yorkshire Television in a repeat of *Only When I Laugh*.

A thriller, *Wait Until Dark*, opened at Bromley the first week of January and is on tour until August, written by Frederick Knott who wrote *Dial M for Murder*. Before we could take off on tour, a letter from the bank brought me down to earth:

Dear Rodney,

For your guidance and attention, I would advise you that your account is overdrawn by £21,142.00 against an agreed limit of £20,000.00.

Yours sincerely . . .

I did like 'for your guidance and attention'.

On the first night of *Wait Until Dark*, Daphne rang the theatre to say my mother was in Lancaster's Royal Albert Infirmary.

It's a big redbrick building with a spire, dominating Lancaster. You can see it from the M6. My mother had trained there as a special nurse when she was Bessie Parkinson from Alfred Street, and she had won a Red Cross medal when she graduated.

I telephoned during the interval of the play and the sister told me my mother had broken a hip and in an Irish accent, 'Ah she's comfortable is all I would say, God bless.'

But then I received a letter from Jane Taylor, the home help, who used to look in on my mother. She told me Mother had lain on the floor all night in pain and couldn't move, cold. She hadn't been wearing her Helpline Call that would've summoned immediate assistance. Jane said my mother had begged her to change her clothes . . . 'I had to tell her I mustn't move her, I said not t'worry, the ambulance men are used to seeing things.'

That morning I was on TV–AM breakfast television to publicise the play. When it was my turn to talk about the tour of *Wait Until Dark* and where we were going after Bromley, Bath, Manchester, Inverness. I thanked the ambulance men who had taken Bessie to the Royal Albert Infirmary instead.

I called the Infirmary every evening during the interval. Daf said my brother had been on the phone raving about me on breakfast television, being the loving son when he has to do everything. Poor Daf said she got cross and had to put the phone down.

I had hardly seen him in thirty years.

I began to dread my nightly call to the hospital. The sister told me, 'I can only say she is very poorly.'

On 14th February, I was to fly to Manchester, then travel on to see my mother who had been moved to a hospice in Grange-over-Sands. At the airport everything started to go wrong. I had been told Terminal Four, but when we got there we were told it was Terminal One. At Terminal One, British Midland said it must be BEA, but they didn't have a booking for me, so I paid for another ticket. I was getting more and more fraught, said goodbye to Daphne on the run and only just caught the plane.

At Manchester, was the hire car Hertz or Avis? Neither had a booking. I had to find my credit cards again. Now I just hoped and prayed the directions to the hospice were clear. It's ninety miles to Barrow-in-Furness. It was dark as I drove north, but I found it all right. Outside the hospice, I parked the car, but didn't want to go in. I walked up and down outside, then when I was shown into my mother's room, didn't recognise her at first and thought I was in the wrong room.

She lay there so tiny, parchment skin, and her tongue out, no speech. I was not even sure she knew me. I sat down.

I wanted her to see me in a suit and Garrick Club tie. I held her hand whilst sitting there, and she looked at me and there was a tiny pressure on my hand and, yes, she was trying to say something. Something like hoar, hoar . . . I began to think she wants Horace, my father . . . I told her stories, smiled and laughed, sitting there holding her hand.

The play opened in Manchester. On the Tuesday, Daphne rang the dressing-room at the Opera House to tell me my mother had died. I thought about how great it was that I had spent Sunday evening with her . . .

I put the phone down and rang my old friend Bill Kenwright, the producer of the tour, who was kind. 'Hang on a sec.' I could hear him shouting across his office. 'His mother's died.' As if they had just been talking about me. 'Go and have a good 'un, kidda. Ring us after, if you want.' It was twenty minutes to curtain up. I was in my dressing-room, looking into the mirror, thinking I must make up.

I was first on. I stood offstage with my hand ready to open the door and found I was shaking. I heard the curtains go up, but I couldn't turn the doorknob . . . the next second I was on, everything was fine and the play took over, Doctor Footlights.

In the interval I rang front of house and ordered a bottle of champagne to take back to my digs.

Ten o'clock the next morning and I was being interviewed yet again. 'What's your favourite episode of *The Likely Lads*? Do you still see your mate? How's Thelma?'

'We're great friends. Had dinner together only last week.'

Relatives were ringing up saying, 'See you next Monday', the day set for the funeral and also when the play would open in Brighton.

I had to ring my brother, who told me, 'I've got it all to do, Rodney.'

It was Monday, 26th February, and there were gales and storms and ninety mile an hour winds. The radio said don't travel and the police said don't travel unless your journey is really necessary. Daphne rang Euston and there were no trains going north and warnings of trees on the line. The 7.20am was cancelled and Euston was in confusion. It was possible to catch a train to Milton Keynes, then a bus to Wolverhampton and then there might be a train north from there. After the funeral, if the 2.30pm to Euston was running it would get in at 5.40, then if I could get the 6.06 to Brighton which got in at 7.11 for curtain up at 7.30 . . . it was impossible!

On opening night in Brighton's Theatre Royal, a huge basket of flowers, an arrangement I think it is called, arrived at the stage door for me from Bill Kenwright, 'Thinking of you, especially today'. Thanks, Boss.

Then at the end of the week in Brighton, Friday night, the stage door man wanted me. There was a crowd of autograph hunters outside. I stepped through the little wooden door and was signing away when a tall man in a mac with metal-framed spectacles pushed through the fans.

'Is is right you didn't go to your mother's funeral?'

How? I just stared at him.

'I'm from the *News of the World*, your brother has spoken to us, to the paper. Would you like to comment? We could go somewhere.'

This in front of people who had been to see the play! All I said was, 'Excuse me, I can't sign any more . . .' I went back inside the theatre. I was in shock. My brother had sold the story. The newspapers would never have known about the funeral, whether I was there or not unless someone had called them with the story. My brother made money from it. That Sunday, this was the whole front page of the *News of the World*:

4th March 1990

LIKELY LAD TOO BUSY FOR MUM'S FUNERAL

Exclusive –

TV STAR Rodney Bewes missed his mother's funeral because he insisted on honouring the stage tradition 'The show must go on'.

But yesterday angry relatives lashed out at the 52-year-old actor. When Bessie Bewes was cremated in Morecambe, Lancs, last week he was busy rehearsing a play in Brighton, 280 miles away.

I wasn't rehearsing. I was playing a play that had my name on the poster. It was sold out because of interviews I had done. And what about the trains not running, trees on the line? And as for angry relatives lashing out, there was just one, my own brother. Auntie Edna, my mother's sister, rang:

'Rodney! Good job your mother was cremated, if she'd been buried she'd be out of that grave today!'

Chapter 28

*T*HE *LIKELY LADS* had not been repeated, not for years. I wrote to all the bosses at the BBC, even to the boss of bosses. I wrote to the director general, the managing director, the controllers of BBC1 and 2, and the head of comedy!

No plans for a repeat of *The Likely Lads* at the moment, but there may come a time . . .
    Best wishes . . .

. . . not possible to repeat the series due to contractual reasons
    Yours sincerely . . .

I had letters from the public about there being no welcome repeats on the TV and from members of the cast too, especially from Cary Ellison, the husband of Olive Milbourne, who played Terry's mother in the series. Cary's letters hinted how welcome a repeat cheque might be. He had been a famous man of the theatre and for thirty years he had looked after actors and their welfare. Now he was writing to me.

. . . can you help, Rodney? We cannot understand why . . .
everything else is on, morning, noon . . . *Dad's Army* is forever
being repeated. Olive sends her love . . .

Should I send him the piece from the *Sunday Times*, 8th January
1989? 'Actors who refuse to allow . . .' 'No longer fitting his
image . . .'

A year after my mother died, I received a letter from her solicitors
requesting me to sign the enclosed and return it. My mother's flat had
been sold. Then that same morning Daphne was whispering in my
ear: 'It's your brother on the phone . . .'

I hadn't spoken to him since before the funeral. Now he wanted
to know if I had signed the papers from the solicitors. He was asking
if I would ring them and say that I had signed them and that they was
in the post. So he could go to their office and collect his half. Then
he added: 'I think we have come out of it rather well.'

'We?'

'How are you doing?'

'Fine.'

'What are you doing? Have you got a lot on?'

'Yes.' I put the phone down.

Dig deep into your humanity, Rodney.

Bill Kenwright sent me a script. It was Beryl Bainbridge's first play,
from a novel of hers, Booker Prize nominated. *An Awfully Big
Adventure* was based on her own experiences in the Fifties at the
Liverpool Playhouse.

I fell in love with Liverpool and the people. Liverpool is one of the
great cities in the world. I guess it is Lancashire and Ireland com-

bined. In the sauna underneath the great Adelphi Hotel, sitting with jockeys slimming for Aintree, I talked to a lady in a one-piece black bathing suit. 'I can't stand the sauna, can you?' I said to her. 'It's so boring. I used to like it when I could read a paper, but I need specs now and of course they steam up.'

'Ah,' she said, 'you can go to an optimist, dey have a spray now and you can spray it on da lenses.'

Great, I thought, I'll go out into the streets of Liverpool – it's full of optimists.

One night, before the play opened, in the Adelphi's great ocean-liner Palm Court lounge, Beryl Bainbridge suddenly jumped up: 'Come on, you've got to see the kitchens.'

We were off on a magical mystery tour of the cavernous kitchens and cellars like the crypt under a gigantic cathedral.

'Now, come on, we've got to find the Aber House Hotel, let's get a taxi.'

The Aber House Hotel featured in the play we were rehearsing. Beryl was like a young girl now, showing me through a taxi window, her Liverpool, the Liverpool of the Fifties before she became a well-known author. 'Stop the taxi, stop here!'

I didn't know where we were, up somewhere past the Philharmonic. Beryl was already out of the cab and knocking on the door.

'Beryl, what are you doing? It's half past one in the morning!'

'This house, see the fanlight? This is the house . . . my husband and I had a club here. He painted the walls like Gauguin, murals on the . . . it was called the Gauguin Club.'

The fanlight above the door lit up, there was someone in the hall. The letterbox flap opened, spilling light. Beryl bent down to look through the letterbox . . .

'Eff off!'

'No, I'm Beryl Bainbridge, just tell me, are there murals on the walls? Gauguin?'

'Eff off!'

'Just want to show my friend . . . in the kitchen, a great mural painting . . . Gauguin?'

'He's not been in tonight!'

The letterbox closed and we were back in the taxi.

Bill Kenwright is director of Everton football club as well as theatre impresario. He asked me: 'Anything you fancy in *Twelfth Night*?' I told him I had always wanted to play Feste, the jester. The director was Gillian Diamond, who had been Peter Hall's casting lady at the National Theatre, but had never directed before. At rehearsals she insisted on giving me line readings, inflections and wanted to discuss the meaning of the lines. One day, she said to do a scene 'As if you are a hostage chained to a radiator in a Beirut cellar.'

This isn't going to work, I thought.

The next morning she put her arm around my shoulder and led me to a corner of the rehearsal room. 'I'm releasing you from the production, Rodney.'

Wow, I'm being fired, I thought.

'It's my fault, Rodney, my Feste is in turmoil inside . . . and you are very still.'

All I could think of was I've got to ring Bill. When I did, he said, 'Hello Butch?'

'Er, boss, I've been fired from *Twelfth Night!*'

'Are you still coming to Arsenal–Everton on Saturday?'

I love him.

Chapter 29

NOW THE 'FOR SALE' board had finally gone up on the house in Cornwall. I thought that if I didn't have the river I'd go potty, well pottier. I was in an antique Thames skiff, up the river, complete with tent and sleeping-bag, when a woman shouted at me from the side of Shiplake lock. 'Oh, Rodney . . .?'

I know we have never met.

'We need someone like you to reopen our theatre, we've got the money for new seating and we need someone like you to come and do a show. You could do whatever you'd like, it's the Kenton in Henley . . .'

I could see the lock gates slowly opening to reveal the long peaceful stretch of water up to Sonning. The other boats were easing out of the lock. I looked up at her. 'No!'

As I skiffed on up towards the upper Shiplake islands I thought with each pull on the blades, what on earth would I do if I opened their theatre? I've never done anything on my own . . . then I knew . . . of course, it's obvious. When I came back through the lock I asked Cliff, the lock-keeper, who the lady was.

'Oh, you want Jean. I'll give her a shout.'

We arranged to meet in Henley at the Little White Hart. Jean from the Kenton Theatre was all excited. I was all excited and I asked her what she thought of my doing *Three Men in a Boat* as a reading? Would the audience feel cheated? No, she didn't think so, she thought it would be unique, so much better than a Variety bill, or . . . and we agreed on a date, 17th September 1993.

The prospect of performing *Three Men in a Boat* scared me. There would be no other turns. Just me. No director, no producer.

I had three old Penguin copies of the book.

I vandalised them to make my script. I wanted ninety minutes: forty-five minutes, interval, forty-five minutes. I had to discard tons of beautiful stuff, but the value of such a one-man show is that you hear the author's words, his sentences. I'm excited. I tried out passages on the stage at Guildford in the afternoons.

I also practised aloud in the open air at Hambledon near the marina, looking at a great cedar tree. There were chickens in the field but they didn't take much interest. Cliff, the lock-keeper, and friends of the Kenton produced a stunning backcloth. I became very apprehensive as the date came nearer.

There was a full house at the gala reopening evening at the Kenton Theatre, New Street. They came in blazers and party dresses and were given Pimm's at the doors. They were noisy, everybody knowing each other. That's a magic noise, backstage.

I came on in London Rowing Club cap and tie, wing collar, green velvet waistcoat and white trousers. I started well, then suddenly, I get to page seven and it isn't there! Panic. Audiences know so quickly if something is wrong. I looked over my specs at them. 'Look, you know what's happened, I know what's happened! Talk amongst yourselves, I'll find it.'

Well, they were laughing and applauding.

'Ah, here it is!'

I knew it was something special in the interval. The audience were spilling out into the street all laughing and talking and piling into the pub opposite.

Losing that page at the beginning had been useful too. It was the same thing as stopping on purpose during a studio TV recording to relax the audience. Show them you are real – they'll eat out of your hand, show them arrogance and they'll go for your throat.

I should write this stuff down.

Jenny Agutter asked me if I would like to do my *Three Men in a Boat* at Cliveden, the great Astor mansion above a wonderful, wooded bend of the river near Maidenhead. Jenny is married to John Tham, the boss of a company that has leased Cliveden from the National Trust and turned it into a grand hotel.

The Hall at Cliveden was a wonderful setting; I stood beside a tall chimney piece, near a large portrait of Nancy Astor. With my stuffed dog under my arm and a wind-up gramophone playing a Twenties jazz record for curtain-up music, I took a moment to stand listening to the music and looking at the sea of friendly faces; the venue, the atmosphere perfect, and I don't think I spoilt it . . . no, it went well, I know it did.

Later I performed at The King's Head pub/theatre, the first professional performance of my *Three Men in a Boat*. It went well, but I knew it needed more work. Tom Courtenay said afterwards, before rushing away: 'No, er, it was . . . as if you didn't know it well enough.'

I keep writing to the BBC about possible repeats of *The Likely Lads* and had a letter back from Michael Jackson, Controller BBC2, a sort of 'all is not lost' letter.

I had another letter from Michael Jackson, inviting me to a 'Thirty Years On' celebration of BBC2 (*The Likely Lads* was one of their first hits in 1964).

I agreed to do my *Three Men in a Boat* at the Garrick Club as a 'Library Talk' and so many of the members subscribed that it was shifted to the morning-room – they couldn't get enough chairs in. A full house. I was very scared, but everyone entered into the spirit of the piece and one famous judge heckled me and got a round of applause. At the dinner afterwards, they were all congratulating me. 'We loved it! Bravo!'

I was at a party at the Television Centre, working the room . . . no, I was not, I was standing about feeling spare until I saw David Attenborough. I talked to him. Three glasses of white wine later, and I was talking to Joan Bakewell. Jeremy Paxman came towards me but saw the Garrick Club tie, his face fell and he retreated. (He had been black-balled.)

I was off in some reverie, when suddenly I was face to face with Michael Jackson, who said, 'We are going to repeat the series in its entirety in the autumn.'

Before I could say anything he was off being greeted by another group. I just stood there with my mouth open. I'd written all those letters, and now I was shell-shocked.

'Would you excuse me?'

I found Michael Jackson again. 'Er, excuse me, would you repeat . . . I, I mean would you, huh, say again what you said to me before?'

'We are going to repeat the series in its entirety in the autumn. *The Likely Lads* first, then *Whatever Happened to the Likely Lads?* next.'

I couldn't wait to tell Daphne. I walked out of the Television

Centre and across the road to White City Tube station and waited for a train. Earl's Court, then a Wimbledon train to take me to Putney and when I walked into the house, Daphne was at the kitchen table. I must have looked awful because she said, 'Oh, Rodney, what's the matter? Have you been in an accident?'

Is that what my face was saying?

'You look, er . . . grey. What is it?'

'Oh, er, Michael Jackson, ever so nice, young, boyish, bright keen, er, the Controller of BBC2. I've written to him.'

'You've written to them all!'

'Said they're going to repeat the series in its entirety in the autumn.'

'Tell me what he said exactly, while I put the kettle on.'

'In its entirety, *The Likely Lads* first, then *Whatever Happened to . . .*, warm and weak and you'd better make it sweet.'

We both sat at the table sipping our tea and looking at each other.

'In the autumn, that's, er, in five months' time, in its entirety, the whole series, the sum total.'

Autumn came and the repeats didn't. I rang Barbara, Michael Jackson's secretary, who told me, 'It's not etched in stone, you know. It might be next year now, possibly January.'

If the series was to be repeated it would come too late for dear Olive Milbourne who played Terry Collier's mother, and whose husband had written to me many times. Sadly, Olive had died before having the fun of seeing them again.

At the end of December, Daphne said, 'You've had an awful two years.'

Only the last two? I thought.

1995 began with no sign of any welcome repeats.

*

I decided to set up a tour of *Three Men in a Boat*, all by myself, no booker. I rang theatres, talked money, everything. My first gig at the aptly named Belfry was cancelled; they wanted Barry Cryer instead.

The advertising agency, Collet Dickinson & Pearce asked me to a party in Soho Square. There was a huge screen on a wall. A show-reel got a great response, a commercial I had made for Bird's Eye Foods twenty years earlier, only shown north of Birmingham. The first line was: 'Hello faggot lovers, everywhere.'

'Do you still see your mate? Funny *The Likely Lads* is never repeated.'

'Oh, yes, only last week . . .' and 'There's been talk at the BBC . . .'

It had been fourteen months since Michael Jackson first raised my hopes. I began to wonder if I had made it up.

On Thursday, 13th July, *The Likely Lads* repeats began on television. We were on the road, taking *Three Men in a Boat* from Glorious Devon to Healthy Harrogate.

On 24th August, a grateful nation had the opportunity to see the first episode of *Whatever Happened to the Likely Lads?* and two weeks later Bill Kenwright rang me to say we had got to number one in the ratings.

In 1996 I was in the West End, first in *Funny Money*, a Ray Cooney farce, and when that ended, four members of the cast were headhunted for *The Odd Couple* at the Haymarket Theatre. As one journalist put it:

Rodney Bewes, Henry McGee, Trevor Bannister and Ron Aldridge snapped up as a job lot from Ray Cooney's *Funny Money* at The Playhouse.

I've never been described as part of a job lot before.

When *The Odd Couple* came off I set my sights on doing my *Three Men in a Boat* again. I had firm dates for 42 venues, and I wanted to do it at the Edinburgh Festival Fringe.

Noreen Taylor wrote in *The Times*: 'Rodney plays three characters with a comic timing that Jack Benny might have envied.'

And in the *Sunday Times*, Jonathan Margolis ended a whole page with: 'It's all a bit homespun for a West End hit yet, like a hand-knitted cardie at a Gaultier show, it could find admirers . . .'

What is so attractive and exciting about the Edinburgh Festival is that hundreds of people, young and old, are performing on every street corner and up alleyways, in rooms above shops, even above Valvona & Crolla! In the dressing-room there's always another performer getting ready or packing up. Terry Neason, actress/singer is pulling and shoving herself into a shiny black plastic basque and I'm trying to put my white trousers on.

'Oh Christ, I'm so fat.'

'Stop it.'

'Oh God, I look dreadful.'

'You look great.'

'I can't go on!'

'You can, you know you can. I've been twice to see you, you're GREAT!'

'I can't do it!'

'Go and kill them. Go, go!'

'I love yer!'

'I love you, GO!'

I had full houses now, every show. I met posh producers who told me they couldn't get in to see me. Nicholas Parsons, Hugh Laurie and Mark Lamarr came to see me, and Paul Merton, and Derek

Nimmo in his Garrick Club tie. I did Saturday, Sunday and every day for three weeks! I didn't mind, I hadn't come here for days off.

A triumph, and I was coming back next year. I had created a show and it was a success.

Chapter 30

THE FOLLOWING YEAR, at Edinburgh in the Assembly Rooms again. I had developed it so that lots of things go wrong on purpose to give it shape and stop it ever becoming a monologue. I strike a match and the lantern comes on in the boat even though I'm a few feet away from it. I indicate the sun on the backcloth and it comes up the other side behind me. A clap of thunder is late and too loud and each time I look to the wings at an imaginary techie who's annoying me more and more.

Every show was sold out again.

On my night off we went to the Russian Circus and a clown fascinated me. He was so sad. He walked around the ring bopping little children on the head with a long rubber floppy French loaf.

'Not PAINFUL!' the second word dragged out in his Russian accent.

'Not PAINFUL,' bop another little head.

Then he is to hit himself. His eyes nearly pop out of his head, as he does so! 'PAINFUL!'

Why, oh why should he grab me so? I went back to see him again. I can hear him now 'Not PAINFUL!'

On another evening, I was standing outside the Assembly Rooms with its three entrance arches topped by four columns up to a pediment. There I was, an old veteran actor Rodney Bewes with an equally old veteran actor Edward Petherbridge.

He said, 'Just look at us, Rodney, at our age . . . on the Fringe!'

After Edinburgh, we were on the road again, towing the 24ft boat, first at Bowhill, a private theatre in the grounds of one of the estates belonging to His Grace, the Duke of Buccleuch and Monmouth. In our hotel Daphne said she found it impossible to call him 'Your Grace'. I said I found it quite easy, after all he was paying our wages.

'Yes, Rodney, but then you've always been an arse-licker.'

I was deeply shocked and still am. What a thing to say. 'Me?'

'Yes, Rodney, and you talk funny to Bill Kenwright too!'

'I do not!'

Dumfries next: the Royal on Shakespeare Street, which dates from 1792, though there are no Georgian bits left. It's been knocked about a bit. But Liz is there to keep the roof on and make tea and look after everything. Every theatre needs a Liz.

Her accent, broad. You know you are in bonny Scotland when talking to Liz. She asked for a prompt copy to follow the play in the wings.

'I don't need a prompter, Liz. Don't prompt, will you?'

'Ock, naa's ust aah's . . . eye ya ken tha . . . follow it!'

I gave her a script and during the show I began to notice a sound from over my right. It was Liz in the wings laughing at the bits coming up. Right, I thought, let's get Liz. So I went blank. What's next? Where am I on the river?

'Liz, what's the next line?'

'Ock, tha muckle hoot ta usta aaaggrht ta Harris, eh, tha noo sed the wee doggie . . .!'

I paused. The audience knew I hadn't forgotten my lines.

'Liz, now do it in English!'

They're cheering and clapping. Liz is obviously very well loved.

One man in my queue at Edinburgh said, 'You know what you ought to do next? *The Diary of a Nobody*, you are Mister Pooter!'

In 2000 I toured *The Diary of a Nobody* to what we might call select venues. The Live Theatre on the Quayside, Newcastle, the Theatre Royal Margate, Cheltenham's Everyman, and the Marine Theatre, Lyme Regis, on my way to Edinburgh Fringe again in August. After I had opened, the first weekend, Bill Kenwright rang me, early one Sunday morning. 'Have you seen the *Sunday Times*, the Culture section?'

'Er, I'm in Edinburgh, boss. I'm standing outside my flat in me pyjamas. I was in er . . .'

'John Peter's given you a rave. Go and get it, no, better still, I'll read it to you:

At the Assembly Rooms . . . Bewes, like the Grossmiths, achieves the seemingly impossible: irresistibly entertaining comedy based on tedium . . . a gem of a performance.

Meanwhile, observe Bewes, alternately solemn and twinkling, both actor and entertainer, handling his audience like a master. It is not, praise the Lord, an intellectual show, but it tells you something quite real about the relationship between actor and the audience – which is where we came in.

At Edinburgh, JOHN PETER.

'A gem of a performance . . . handling his audience like a master' – thanks John Peter.

So here I am going back to Edinburgh this summer, back to the Assembly Rooms to do my *Three Men in a Boat* for a third time. I hope Jerome K Jerome would have approved of this, my poor book. He said about his most famous book:

> What readers ask nowadays in a book is that it should improve, instruct and elevate. This book wouldn't elevate a cow.

At the end of my show in Edinburgh, and on the road, I make a curtain speech, though it differs from venue to venue:

> Thank you, thank you, thank you, on behalf of the *entire* company. Thank you! I have been asked by the management, a somewhat euphemistic term for them, to say the circle bar is still open. If you are not in a hurry to catch your last bus or climb into your Range Rover Discovery, you are welcome to come on stage and look at my boat, built by Messums of Richmond in 1911. If you are upset now that you didn't buy a programme, to place in a sock drawer and one day sell it at Sotheby's or Christie's for a fortune, don't worry – I take a tray of books and programmes to the bar where I *sell* them at a small profit, and sign them at no extra charge! If you don't come to the bar I will understand, for I am told it can be very daunting to meet someone really . . . famous!

Final bow.